LIFE SKILLS
ACTIVITIES
FOR SPECIAL
CHILDREN

LIFE SKILLS ACTIVITIES FOR SPECIAL CHILDREN

Darlene Mannix

illustrated by Carrie Oesmann

THE CENTER FOR APPLIED
RESEARCH IN EDUCATION

Library of Congress Cataloging-in-Publication Data

Mannix, Darlene.
    Life skills activities for special children / Darlene Mannix ;
illustrated by Carrie Oesmann.
       p. cm.
    ISBN 0-87628-547-7
    1. Mentally handicapped children–United States–Life skills
guides.   2. Life skills–Study and teaching (Elementary)–United
States.   I. Title.
HV894.M36   1991   95-21805
371.91–dc20   CIP

Printed in the United States of America

11 12 13 14 15 16 17 18 19 20

ISBN 0-87628-547-7

ATTENTION: CORPORATIONS AND SCHOOLS

The Center for Applied Research in Education books are available at quantity discounts
with bulk purchase for educational, business, or sales promotional use. For information,
please write to: Prentice Hall Special Sales, 240 Frisch Court, Paramus, New Jersey
07652. Please supply: title of book, ISBN number, quantity, how the book will be used,
date needed.

**THE CENTER FOR APPLIED RESEARCH
IN EDUCATION**

On the World Wide Web at http://www.phdirect.com

THIS BOOK IS DEDICATED TO

Jim Pantos
principal of Boston Middle School
in La Porte, Indiana
and
Steve Manering
assistant principal of Boston Middle School
for all we've been through together;

and to

Mom, Dad, Ben, Jennifer, and Kara.

ABOUT THE AUTHOR

Darlene Mannix has been a teacher of many categories and ages of students, including the emotionally disturbed, learning disabled, multiply mentally handicapped, at-risk, and language disordered. She holds a Bachelor of Science degree from Taylor University and a Master's degree in learning disabilities from Indiana University. She is presently teaching a pilot program for middle school students utilizing computers to teach thinking skills.

Ms. Mannix's other publications include *Oral Language Activities for Special Children* (1987, The Center for Applied Research in Education) and *Be a Better Student: Lessons and Worksheets for Teaching Behavior Management in Grades 4–9* (1989, The Center for Applied Research in Education).

ABOUT THIS BOOK

The purpose of *Life Skills Activities for Special Children* is to provide you with a collection of practical, easy-to-use, open-ended activities to assist in teaching life skills to special children. Many types of skills are required today, not only to survive but to experience independence and success in everyday living. Special children, in particular, need extra help in focusing on learning tasks that have been identified to help them become more independent in their homes, at school, and in their community.

The format of the lessons is easy to follow. The objective of the lesson, discussion ideas, worksheet instructions, and extension ideas are clearly laid out for you to follow or adapt as you see fit for the class. The topics selected range from skills needed for basic survival to those that will enhance the child's leisure time and ability to get around the community to pursue interests.

While the material could easily be used as a social studies curriculum for younger children, portions could supplement current events for older children, oral discussion or thinking time, social skills training, as well as specific academic needs such as vocabulary enrichment or reading.

Audience

The lessons are primarily intended for upper-elementary-aged students with special learning needs. While skills such as reciting one's name and address are quite elementary, this book focuses on placing the specific skill within the context of real-life situations. *When* would you reveal your name and address? *Why* is it important to know who your doctor is and what medications you are taking? While this information may be obvious to most children, the special children for whom this is directed need the extra focus of understanding how to fit into the real world and how to develop the skills that they will need to become independent of their parents, sheltered home, and/or protection of school. Special children want to gain the freedom that their regular education counterparts are achieving. They want to become familiar with their community, know how to perform certain tasks on their own, and be able to enjoy leisure activities safely and thoroughly. Special children need to focus on particular, targeted skills, with extra time and practice allotted for mastery of that skill. Using the behavioral objective as the initial step, you can direct the children through the activities, supplementing the worksheet pages with applications from the youngsters' own home or community.

Because special children need a good language/thinking experience prior to acquiring a concept, each skill is introduced with a short discussion of related questions. The worksheets then focus on a particular aspect of the skill and provide, by example, problem-solving activities or completion exercises linking the skill with the situation in which it is likely to be encountered. Many of the activities are open-ended so that appropriate applications can be made for the specific child or class.

Special Features

Each lesson is introduced with a specific *objective*, suitable for special education plans. The *worksheet activities* can be reproduced for classroom use. Children may wish to color the pictures, display them around the room, and certainly take them home to discuss with their parents. Also included are periodic *letters to parents* which inform the adults at home about specific skills that are being taught. Suggestions for parental involvement to reinforce the skills at home are also given. A *skill sheet* is provided for each section of skills and can be used by you for periodic monitoring of the acquisition of skills which may take time to develop, or a grade-book method of checking off when a lesson has been satisfactorily completed.

Content

The general scope of the workbook is to expose the child to many varied types of skills needed for independent living. These skills include basic personal living skills as well as social skills.

Part I—Basic Survival Skills: This section focuses on teaching skills required for a child to survive and protect himself or herself. Special children in particular need to be able to communicate information about themselves, demonstrate some degree of proficiency with using a telephone, understand and appropriately handle situations involving money, have some familiarity with time concepts, read and understand community words and signs, and develop coping strategies for handling everyday stress.

Part II—Personal Independence: The greatest task a special child may face is that of acquiring independence for himself or herself on what may appear to be simple, ordinary activities. This section targets skills of appropriate dressing and care of clothing, keeping oneself clean, maintaining a clean room, obtaining food and other related tasks, creating an awareness of a healthy lifestyle, and exploring situations specific to latch-key children. The life skills highlighted in this section will be of particular interest to parents, who may be the primary caregivers of these skills. Teachers working in conjunction with interested parents can set forth a systematic plan for teaching these basic life skills to special children.

Part III—Community Independence: Special children are members of a community, and therefore they are entitled to use the resources it may offer. A new set of life skills is appropriate for children who are aware of their community and can learn to be an active part of it. This section focuses on establishing an awareness of community places and people, specific use of resources in the community, behavior expected of children in public, and issues of getting around safely in the community and provides information that may help the child to become familiar with his or her community.

Part IV—Getting Along with Others: As the special child becomes increasingly more independent, his or her world expands, and, likewise, the skills required for successful functioning grow more complex and involve more people. This section exposes the child to a world filled with people, diverse in many ways. Other skills include developing an awareness of the need to cooperate with others, understand another's point of view, and demonstrate good manners in many different situations.

A Final Word

By using typical, everyday situations that a child would encounter, the lessons provide the children with opportunities to learn about, practice, and apply life skills in a controlled situation, preparing them for eventually exercising the skills in real-life situations.

Darlene Mannix

CONTENTS

LIFE SKILLS ACTIVITIES FOR SPECIAL CHILDREN

part I

Basic
Survival
Skills

PARENT LETTER #1   RELATING
BASIC INFORMATION

Dear Parents,

In the next few weeks, we will be discussing and practicing telling basic information about ourselves, such as name, address, phone number, date of birth, family members, and emergency needs. This is not intended to be an intrusion into your private lives, but it is important for your child to be able to identify these items about himself or herself. It would help me a lot to have the correct answers so that I can make sure your child is learning the right information! Please help by completing the form at the bottom of this page and return by _____ . You can also help by practicing this information with your child at home.

Thanks for your help!

Sincerely,

_____
Teacher

- -

Child's Name: _____   Date of birth: _____

Parents: (father's name) _____   (mother's name) _____

Who lives in the home: _____

Address: _____

Phone number: _____

Where parents work: (father) _____   (mother) _____

Phone number at work: (father) _____   (mother) _____

Emergency or medical needs: _____

3

I-A RELATING BASIC INFORMATION

Skill Sheet #1: Progress Report

+ mastered
√ emerging
− not mastered

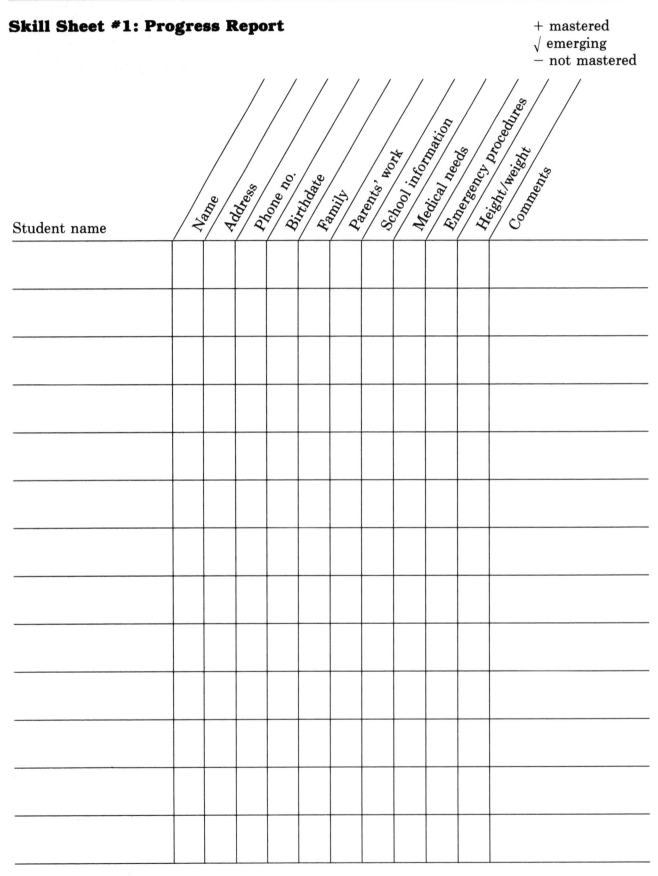

Student name	Name	Address	Phone no.	Birthdate	Family	Parents' work	School information	Medical needs	Emergency procedures	Height/weight	Comments

I-A RELATING BASIC INFORMATION   *LESSON 1*

WHO ARE YOU?

Objective:

Upon request or in appropriate situations, the student will state his or her full name.

Discussion:

Teacher: Were any of you named after your parents or a particular person? Is there a name that is special for some reason in your family? Names are very important. Can you help me list reasons why someone might need to know your name? (if you're lost, filling out a form, etc.)

Worksheet I-1 On this worksheet, you will see four examples of when you should tell someone your name. I want you to listen while I read the directions, and then finish drawing the student to resemble yourself. In the cartoon "balloon," write how you would tell someone your name.

Answers (examples):

1. Yes, the card should say (name).
2. My name is (name).
3. My whole name is (name).
4. I'm (name).

Extension Activities:

1. **Name Meanings.** Locate a baby name book and have students look up what their first name means. If students know, have them tell the origin of their given name as well as their last name.
2. **Name Posters.** Have students draw and color posters using the letters of their names. Students may shape the letters to form a picture of something that interests them (e.g., a skateboard, airplane).

WHO ARE YOU?

Pretend that you are the student in each picture below. Fill in the cartoon to tell how you would answer each person in each situation.

1.

2.

3.

4.

I-A RELATING BASIC INFORMATION   *LESSON 2*

WHERE I LIVE

Objective:

Upon request or in appropriate situations, the student will state or write his or her address.

Discussion:

Teacher: What kind of mail comes to your house? How does the mail carrier know where to deliver everything? If you were going to send away for something, what information would you need to give the people who were going to send it to you? Your *address* is the directions for where you live. Usually your address includes house number, street, city, state, and zip code. You will need to know all of these parts of your address.

Worksheet I-2 It is important for everyone to know his or her complete address. On this worksheet help the students find the missing parts of their address. Then we will work on the directions for your address, including all of the same information.

Answers:

1. State—Indiana
2. City—Milwaukee
3. House number—307
4. Street—Lemon Grove Parkway
5. Zip code—22901

Extension Activities:

1. **Roll Your Address.** Using one die, have students roll and state the part of their address indicated by the following key: one—house number, two—street, three—city, four—state, five—zip code, six—roll again.

2. **My House.** Have students draw or color and cut out a paper house (or apartment, trailer, etc.) with the appropriate information on it. Have students send a letter through the mail to another student using the address from the paper house. When the letter is received, have the student bring it to school and display it next to his or her paper house.

WHERE I LIVE

Something is missing from each of the following addresses. Help the student figure out the missing part and use the Help Box at the bottom to complete the address. Write the answer on the line.

1. 507 East Main Street
   Bloomington _____ 47401   _____

2. 300 N. 7th Street
   _____ Wisconsin 53213   _____

3. _____
   Washington Street
   La Porte, Indiana 46350   _____

4. 1074 _____
   Englewood Cliffs, New Jersey 07632   _____

5. Box 330, Route 7
   Charlottesville, Virginia _____   _____

```
┌─ HELP BOX ─────────────────────────────────────────────┐
│                                                          │
│      307          Lemon Grove Parkway        22901       │
│                                                          │
│            Indiana              Milwaukee                │
│                                                          │
└──────────────────────────────────────────────────────────┘
```

HELLO, ANYBODY HOME?

Objective:

Upon request or in appropriate situations, the student will state his or her phone number.*

Discussion:

Teacher: Just last night I talked to a friend of mine who lives 100 miles away. How did I do that? (via phone) What do you need to know to make a phone call? Why might it be important to know your phone number?

Worksheet I-3 Think about why people would need to know your phone number. On this sheet, you will decide whether or not someone needs to reach you by phone, and you will write down your phone number when it is needed.

Answers:

1. Yes
2. Yes (although it could be mailed)
3. No
4. Yes (discuss area codes)
5. No
6. Yes

Extension Activities:

1. **Class Phone Book.** If there are no objections from parents or school administrators, compile a class phone/address book. You may want to include other information as well, such as birthdates, pets, favorite activities, and so on.†

2. **Call Me.** With prior parent notification, have students assigned to partners within the class. Inform students that they need to state/write their phone number correctly so that their partner can call him or her on a designated evening. Have students ask specific questions of each other over the phone and discuss the responses at school the following day.

---

*If students do not have a phone in their home, do not embarrass them or pry into reasons why they do not have a phone. Also, some students may have an unlisted number which they cannot divulge. You may adapt this activity by having them learn a parent's number (see Lesson 6) or other emergency number.

†Be sure that releasing this information is okay with all parties involved.

HELLO, ANYBODY HOME?

Which of these people would need to know your phone number to tell you something? Write *yes* or *no* on the line next to each situation. If it is *yes*, write your phone number too.

1. Mr. Pierce wants you to know that football practice has been canceled because of the rain. _____

2. You just won a free trip to Hawaii! The lady from the travel agency has the details. _____

3. Your best friend mailed you a birthday card. _____

4. Your aunt in France wants to wish you happy birthday. _____

5. Your next-door neighbor dropped off flowers for you while you were sick. _____

6. A friend wants to let you know what time everyone is going to go bowling. _____

I-A RELATING BASIC INFORMATION   *LESSON 4*

HAPPY BIRTHDAY TO ME!

Objective:

Upon request or in appropriate situations, the student will state his or her birthdate.

Discussion:

Teacher: Do you know this song? (hum the "Happy Birthday to You" tune) What does it mean? What is a birthday? When someone asks for your *birthdate,* they want to know the month, day, and year that you were born. Why would someone need to know how old you are? (movie tickets, reduced meal rates, class at school, etc.)

Worksheet I-4 Here are some examples of people wanting to know some dates. Not all of them need to know your birthdate, however. I want you to figure out which ones need to know the date you were born.

Answers:

1. Yes   4. No
2. No   5. Yes
3. Yes

Extension Activities:

1. **Everybody with This Month Game.** For practice in recognizing their birthdates, have students stand up/touch their toes/turn around, and so on if they have a birthdate in a specific month. Go through the months in random order and at a fast pace!

2. **Birthdate Helpers.** When you need a classroom helper, instead of drawing the student's name from a hat, use their birthdates. ("I need someone with the birthdate of October 16, 1980 to run an errand for me.")

_____

HAPPY BIRTHDAY TO ME!

The people shown on this worksheet want to know some dates from 🎂 you. Draw a birthday cake if they want to know your birthdate, and write the date on the line. If it is another date that they want, leave the line blank.

1. I want to get you a wonderful birthday present! When were you born?

2. When did you have your last dentist appointment?

3. Are you old enough to ride the bumper cars? How old are you?

4. Your mother looks so young! What is her birthdate?

5. I think we were born in the same month and the same year. Tell me your birthdate.

I-A RELATING BASIC INFORMATION *LESSON 5*

MY FAMILY

Objective:

Upon request or in appropriate situations, the student will name the members of his or her family.

Discussion:

Teacher: How many of you have a brother or sister? Who else is in your family? Is a pet dog a family member? There are many ways to describe what a family is. It could be the people you live with, people who take care of each other, or people who are related to each other. We are going to say that a *family* is a group of people who are together in some way. If we talk about your home family, that will mean the people who live at your house. There may be people who are related to you who do not usually live at your house. Those people are part of your family too, but not your home family.

Worksheet I-5 Today you are going to match some students with their home families. Read the clues and see if you can figure out which family the student is from. Match the family group with the student, and write the letter on the line.

Answers:

1. Mary—D
2. Marcos—B
3. Frank—E
4. Kelly—A
5. David—C

Extension Activities:

1. **Family Portrait.** Have students draw or bring in pictures of family members. They may wish to portray their natural family if this differs from the people who live in their home. They should feel free to include a divorced parent and siblings who do not live in their home. Use a loose definition of "family" for this activity. Have students introduce their families to each other.

2. **Family Awards.** Have a designated Family Day and give awards for the student with the most siblings, youngest sibling, tallest mother, newest in town, and so on. Students may wish to award their own families with some unique attribute they know about.

MY FAMILY

Here are some students who are describing their families. Match each student with the group that is his or her family. Write the letter assigned to that group on the line by the student.

1. Mary

   I have a big brother, John, and two little sisters, Sandy and Jane. I live with my mother and my grandmother. That's my family!

   Ⓐ

   _____

2. Marcos

   I have a little baby sister and an older sister. We live with my father and my stepmother.

   Ⓑ

   _____

3. Frank

   My parents are divorced. I spend the week with my mother and stepfather. My stepfather has one son. I don't have any other brothers or sisters.

   Ⓒ

   _____

4. Kelly

   I live with my mother and my aunt. I have one sister. There are alot of women at my house.

   Ⓓ

5. David

   My parents are away so while they are gone my family is my Aunt Carol and Uncle John. They don't have any other kids.

   Ⓔ

   _____ _____

© 1992 by The Center for Applied Research in Education

I-A RELATING BASIC INFORMATION   *LESSON 6*

MY PARENTS AND WHERE THEY ARE

Objective:

Upon request or in appropriate situations, the student will state where his or her parents can be reached.

Discussion:

Teacher: Have you ever known of anyone who got hurt or sick at school? What happened? (called a parent) What would happen to you if you had an accident at school? How could your parents be reached?

Worksheet I-6 All your students need to reach their parents or person who can help them. Some of them know enough information to get through, and some of them don't. Write *yes* or *no* if the student could or could not locate his or her parent or guardian with the information given. Then we will discuss what we could do here if we needed to get in touch with someone at your house if there was an emergency or important situation.

Answers:

1. No (needs to know which hospital)
2. Yes
3. Yes
4. No (needs to know work schedule)
5. No (needs work phone number)

Extension Activities:

1. **Backup Plan.** Have students individually relate what procedure should be followed if the parents needed to be contacted in an emergency. Although this information should be on an emergency card in the school office, students should be able to state the names of a neighbor, friend, or relative who could be called upon if necessary.

2. **School Nurse.** Have students role play situations in which one has an ailment (they can be creative as to the various maladies) and the other is the "school nurse." Have students practice giving appropriate information clearly and completely.

MY PARENTS AND WHERE THEY ARE

These students need to get in touch with their parents. Some of them do not know the information to contact them. If students have enough information, write *yes* on the line. If they need more information, write *no* on the line.

1. My leg really hurts. Could you call my dad!? He works at the hospital, but I don't remember which one.

_____

2. I forgot my math book! It has all of my homework in it! My mother is at home and our phone number is 367-2440.

_____

3. It's raining — I wonder if my stepfather can pick me up after school. Let's see... he works at Smith's Service Station and the number is 274-3093.

_____

4. I need to tell my grandmother about the meeting at school tonight. I know she's at her job, but I don't know if she works today or not.

_____

5. I'm supposed to call dad when I'm ready to come home. My home number is 324-5827 but dad's at work right now.

_____

I-A RELATING BASIC INFORMATION   *LESSON 7*

MEET MY TEACHER

Objective:

Upon request or in appropriate situations, the student will state the name of his or her teacher, grade or class in school, and/or the name of the school he or she attends.

Discussion:

Teacher: Pretend you have a friend from far away who is coming to visit you for a day at school. What information would you need to give him or her so that you could be located? Why do you think it is important to know the name of your teacher? (so someone would know what class you're in)

Worksheet I-7 Here are some students who need to know the name of their teacher and what grade they are in. Use the clues to figure out whose class they are in. Write your answers on the lines.

Answers:

    1. Mrs. Martin
    2. Miss Alexander
    3. Mr. King
    4. Mrs. Martin
    5. Mrs. Martin
    6. Mr. King
    7. Miss Alexander
    8. Miss Alexander
    9. Mr. King (some assumptions were made here)
  10. Miss Alexander

Extension Activities:

1. **Teacher Hall of Fame.** Locate pictures of all the teachers in your school. Assign students to find out the names, grades or classes taught by the teachers. Put that and other interesting information on posters and arrange them for display.

2. **Guest Visitor.** Have teachers drop in for a five-minute interview by your class. Assign students to prepare some questions for the teacher. Teachers may wish to display or tell something interesting about themselves to share with your class as well.

MEET MY TEACHER

These are students from the classes of Mr. King, who teaches fourth grade, Mrs. Martin, who teaches fifth grade, and Miss Alexander, who teaches sixth grade. Help the students get to the right class. Write the name of the teacher next to the student who is in his or her class.

Mr. King

Mrs. Martin

Miss Alexander

1. Jason is in fifth grade this year.   _____

2. Mark was in fifth grade last year.   _____

3. Jenny likes having a man for a teacher.   _____

4. Kim had Mr. King last year.   _____

5. Fred does not have Miss Alexander or a man for a
   teacher.   _____

6. Ramon has to repeat fourth grade this year.   _____

7. Angel has the same teacher that Mark has.   _____

8. Zac is a year ahead of Jason in school.   _____

9. Kara's teacher is not married. Kara is not in sixth
   grade.   _____

10. Karin was in fourth grade two years ago.   _____

I-A RELATING BASIC INFORMATION   *LESSON 8*

MEDICAL NEEDS

Objective:

Upon request or in appropriate situations, the student will state what medication or medical needs he or she requires.

Discussion:

Teacher: Sometimes people need special medication to help themselves stay healthy. Can any of you give some examples of why special medicine may be required? (seizure control, blood pressure, etc.) *Medication* is a big word that refers to the medicine that a doctor has told you to take. It is not the same thing as taking drugs in a bad way. This is something that assists a person who needs extra help. Why is it important for someone to be able to tell what medication he or she needs? (to get help in a hurry) Suppose someone needs immediate *medical attention.* Can you think of any examples? (nosebleeds, seizures) How do glasses help someone?

Worksheet I-8 Here are a few examples of students who have specific medical needs. Read about their situations and decide what the best thing to do is in each case. Circle the letter of the best answer. Then we'll discuss your choices.

Answers:

1. d
2. a
3. c

Extension Activities:

1. **School Nurse Visit.** Invite the school nurse to stop in and explain some basic medical situations and how they are handled, such as the need to wear glasses, epilepsy, or specific handicaps. Emphasize that medication or medical advice is to be followed specifically.

2. **Book Reports.** Check out books from your school or local library dealing with children who have specific medical conditions, such as diabetes or leukemia. Read them to your class or have capable students do book reports on them and discuss as a class.

MEDICAL NEEDS

Each of the following students has a medical need. Show what that student should do by circling the best answer in each story.

1. Kim often gets nosebleeds at school. Her mother told her to pinch her nose tightly when it bleeds. The next time it happens, what should Kim do?
    a. Call her mother and go home from school.
    b. Let her teacher know.
    c. Rush to the bathroom with several friends.
    d. Pinch her nose.

2. Randy needs to take a pill every day after lunch to control his seizures. One day he realized that he didn't have any pills left in the office. What should he do?
    a. Let the school nurse know to call home.
    b. Hope that he doesn't have a seizure.
    c. Take someone else's pill.
    d. Go home.

3. Jeff had an operation on his leg and is supposed to keep his leg raised for a few hours each afternoon. One afternoon he wanted to play outside with his friends. What should he do?
    a. Call his doctor and ask if he can go out this time.
    b. Tell his teacher that it is ok to go out.
    c. Keep his leg raised.
    d. Have his friends play football inside the classroom.

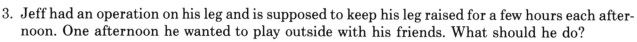

I-A RELATING BASIC INFORMATION *LESSON 9*

EMERGENCY!

Objective:

The student will recognize an emergency situation and follow appropriate procedures.

Discussion:

Teacher: What is an ambulance for? (to help in emergency situations, accidents) Who are the people on board the ambulance? What kind of training do you think they have to have? An *emergency* is a situation that needs attention right away. Can you give me some examples of emergencies? (accident, fire, etc.) Unless you know exactly what to do, it is best to call someone who can help with the situation. Who are some people you can call? (adults, police, firefighter, doctor, etc.)

Worksheet I-9 Here are some examples of emergency situations and some students who have ideas as to what to do. Decide in each case which students are doing the best thing. We will discuss your answers.

Answers:

1. A
2. C
3. B

Extension Activities:

1. **Red Cross.** The Red Cross publishes numerous easy-to-understand pamphlets dealing with basic first aid and emergency situations. As a class project, list common emergency situations and come up with viable solutions. You may wish to show a filmstrip or video on basic first aid. Be sure students are aware of their limitations. (CPR, for example, should only be performed by trained persons.)

2. **Larry the Loser.** Have students write a silly story about a careless person who gets into dangerous situations (walking down the middle of a street, throwing matches around, etc.) and causes numerous emergencies. Invent a superhero ("Carlos the Careful"??) who teaches Larry some safety skills. Identify the emergencies created and appropriate action to be taken in each.

EMERGENCY!

Here are some situations that need attention right away. Circle the letter assigned to the student who you think is doing the best thing.

1. **Situation:** There is smoke coming from the trash can in your garage.

2. **Situation:** A strange dog bit a little girl on the arm.

3. **Situation:** Your friend fell while playing and his head is bleeding.

I-A RELATING BASIC INFORMATION   *LESSON 10*

MY VITAL STATISTICS

Objective:

Upon request or in appropriate situations, the student will state his current height and weight.

Discussion:

Teacher: How tall do you think I am? How much do you think I weigh? Well, I'm not going to tell you how much I weigh, but I bet you can tell me how to find out. What tools could you use to find out these things? (scale, height chart, etc.) Why is it important to know how tall you are? (buying clothes, getting into rides at the fair) Why is it important to know how much you weigh? (monitoring health, staying in shape) Your *height* is how tall you are in feet and inches. Your *weight* is how many pounds you weigh on a scale.

Worksheet I-10 This worksheet shows four students and their heights and weights. Sometimes rides and exhibits at fairs have restrictions or limits for your height and weight. Write the names of the students who could go on the rides or exhibits shown on the worksheet.

Answers:

1. Fred, Jason
2. Sandy, Maria
3. None
4. Sandy, Maria
5. Sandy, Fred, Maria

Extension Activities:

1. **My Height and Weight.** Take your students to the nurse's office and have each measured and weighed. Have them write the numbers on a picture or drawing of themselves. If you do this at the beginning of the year, repeat the activity after a few months to note changes.

2. **My Day at the Fair.** After students know their height and weight, have them figure out which rides or exhibits they could participate in using the worksheet!

I-10

MY VITAL STATISTICS

Here are the numbers for the height and weight of some students. Write the names of the students who could do the activities shown on the lines below the pictures.

Sandy    Fred    Jason    Maria

Height: 4 ft. 3 in.   5 ft. 1 in.   5 ft. 11 in.   4 ft. 1½ in.
Weight: 75 lbs.   100 lbs.   130 lbs.   67 lbs.

1. Roller Coaster

You must be at least 5 feet tall to ride this ride!

_____

2. Swinging Bridge

You'll go on this if you weigh more than 90 pounds!

Don't go on this if you weigh more than 90 pounds!

_____

3. Fun House

Only people shorter than 4 feet can go in the Fun House!

_____

4. Teeter-Totter

This is for people under 80 pounds!

_____

5. Narrow Pass

You'll get stuck if you weigh more than 120 pounds!

_____

Dear Parents,

A very important survival skill for our children to learn is that of making and receiving telephone calls. Our next unit of study deals with dialing phone numbers, giving and receiving messages over the phone, taking a message for someone else, using a pay telephone, and becoming familiar with the local phone book (White and Yellow Pages). Some of the activities your child may ask you to help with include making phone calls at home to another member of the class, paging through your phone book in search of information, and taking messages at home. Please allow your child supervised access to your telephone, if possible.

Thanks!

Sincerely,

_____

Teacher

I-B TELEPHONE SKILLS

Skill Sheet #2: Progress Report

+ mastered
√ emerging
− not mastered

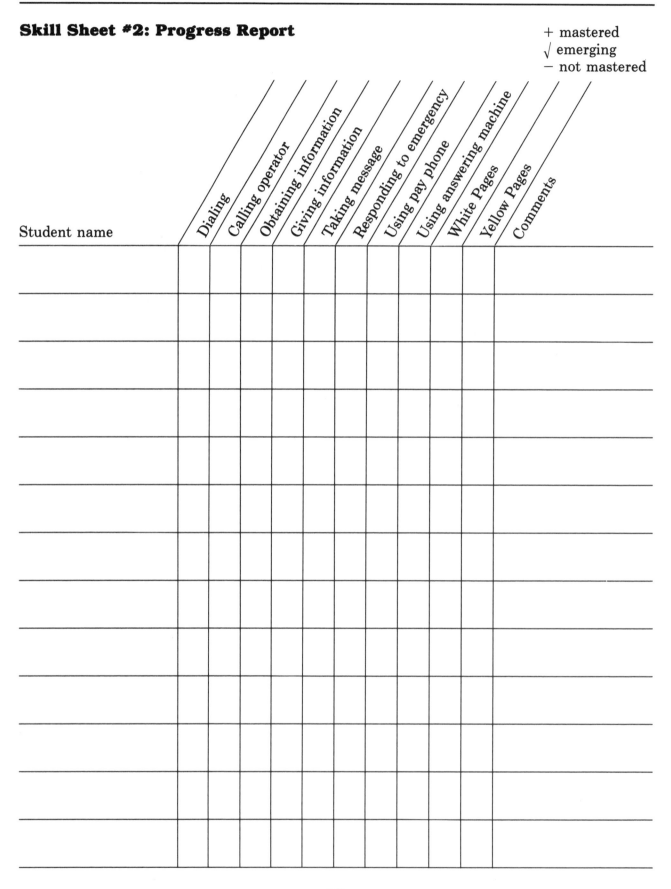

Student name	Dialing	Calling operator	Obtaining information	Giving information	Taking message	Responding to emergency	Using pay phone	Using answering machine	White Pages	Yellow Pages	Comments

DIALING THE NUMBER

Objective:

Given a number, the student will correctly dial/depress the numbers on a telephone.

Discussion:

Teacher: Who can tell me your phone number? If I wanted to call you at home, how would I do that? (dial the numbers) Does anyone know the two basic types of phones? A *touch-tone phone* has buttons that you press. A *rotary dial phone* has a wheel that you turn in a circle. What kind of phone do you have in your home?

Worksheet I-11 These pages show the two types of phones: touch tone and rotary dial. You are going to practice dialing or punching in the numbers you see at the top. Later we will do this with real phones and real phone numbers. Remember, you don't have to press too hard or too fast; do each number carefully. Check off each number when you are done. (You may want to have students work in partners to make sure they are doing this carefully and accurately.)

Extension Activities:

1. **Phone Log.** Use the class phone book (Lesson 3) and have students assigned to call a partner with a brief message for several evenings. Have students make a note of what the message that was called in by the other student was about.

2. **Practice Calls.** Have students call local numbers with parent supervision. (No 800 or 900 #'s) In my class, one student was selected each day to find out the weather report by calling the local bank for the recorded message.

DIALING THE NUMBER

The first page shows a touch-tone phone. The second page shows a rotary dial phone. Show how you would dial the phone numbers on both types of phones. Check off each number when you have finished.

1. 324-5827 _____   4. 788-2387 _____

2. 871-3992 _____   5. 632-8114 _____

3. 641-0044 _____   6. 322-0388 _____

Touch-Tone Phone

1. 324-5827 _____

2. 871-3992 _____

3. 641-0044 _____

4. 788-2387 _____

5. 632-8114 _____

6. 322-0388 _____

Rotary Dial Phone

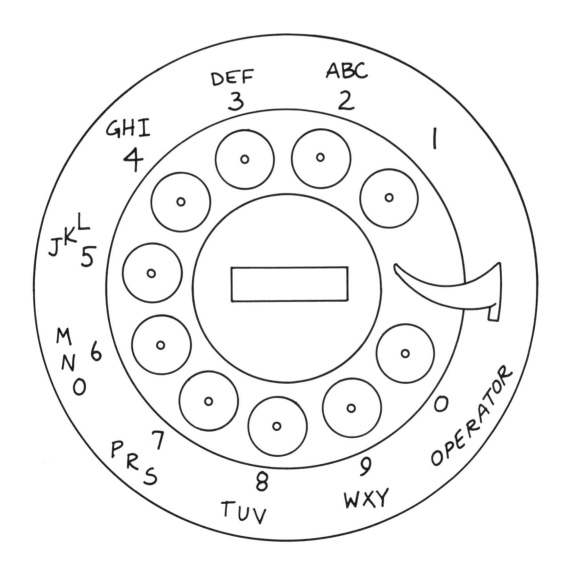

O IS FOR OPERATOR

Objective:

The student will recognize that the "0" on the phone will connect him or her with an operator and that this service should be used for specific situations.

Discussion:

Teacher: Does anyone know what the "0" on the telephone is for? What will happen if that is the only number you dial? (reach the operator) The *operator* is a person who will help you make your phone call. Why don't we just call the operator every time you want to make a call? (too time consuming, not necessary) When should you use the operator to help you? (having trouble completing call, in an emergency, et cetera)

Worksheet I-12 Here are some situations where someone wants to make a phone call. Decide whether or not you should use the operator to help you make the call. Keep in mind that you should use the operator only when it is an emergency, or when you are having a problem with the phone, or when you need more information. Don't bother the operator if you can figure it out by yourself. Write *yes* or *no* on the line after each situation.

Answers:

1. No	6. Yes
2. Yes	7. Yes
3. No—if you can look it up	8. Yes
4. No	9. Yes
5. No	10. No

Extension Activities:

1. **May I Help You?** Have students take turns role playing an operator and people with specific questions or problems. Include some emergency situations as well as routine information. Students should have fun with this, but realize when it is appropriate to use the operator.

2. **Operator.** Have students use the operator's assistance on one supervised instance so that they are familiar with the procedure.

O IS FOR OPERATOR

Tell if you think you should call the operator in these situations. Write *yes* or *no* on the line.

1. You dialed your phone number three times, and each time it is busy. _____

2. You want to call a friend who just moved to town, and his number isn't in the phone book yet. _____

3. You want to call your neighbor but you don't know her number. _____

4. You are supposed to call your dad at work and you are too tired to look up his number in the phone book. _____

5. You are bored and want to talk to someone about your day. _____

6. You think there is a fire in the house. _____

7. You dialed a phone number but you keep getting cut off. _____

8. Your friend moved away and you aren't sure of his new phone number. _____

9. The telephone keeps buzzing every time you dial the number. _____

10. You call your friend, but she is not home and the phone just keeps ringing. _____

OBTAINING INFORMATION

Objective:

The student will use an appropriate source to obtain information about a specific situation.

Discussion:

Teacher: If you wanted to find out what the weather is going to be like, how could you use the phone? Would you call the operator? (no, use prerecorded service) What if you wanted to find out a friend's number if that person moved to another city? The phone company offers a service called *directory assistance* that will give you phone numbers without using the operator. (Check with your local phone company to determine the procedure.) What are some other numbers you can call for information?

Worksheet I-13 Here are some situations where people need to call for information about something. Match each situation with the source that will help them out. Write the letter on the line.

Answers:

1. e	5. g
2. d	6. h
3. f	7. a
4. b	8. c

Extension Activities:

1. **I Want to Know.** Have students list three questions that they want to find out about (similar to those on the worksheet). Have them exchange questions and work on each others situations to find an appropriate source to find the answer.

2. **Now I Know.** As a follow-up to the first activity, have students actually call one of their sources to find out the answer (a time, a place, a quantity, etc.).

Name _____ Date _____

I–13

OBTAINING INFORMATION

The students want to find out some information using the phone. Match each student with the source that will help them find out what they want to know. Write the letter on the line following each situation.

1. Alex wants to know what the weather will be like this afternoon. _____

2. Bridget wants to know the phone number of a friend who just moved to a new city. _____

3. Carl wants to know what time the zoo opens on Saturday. _____

4. Tara wants to order a pizza. _____

5. Michael wants to call his favorite radio station to ask them to play his favorite song. _____

6. Randy wants to know if the bike he ordered has come in yet. _____

7. Debbie wants to know if the library has the latest mystery story by her favorite author. _____

8. Keith and Chad can't wait to see the horror movie at the local theater, but don't know what time it starts.

_____

a. Greenville Public Library

b. Hank's Pizza Store

c. Town and Country Movies

d. Directory assistance

e. Local weather

f. Westville Zoo

g. WZQD radio station

h. Center Street Sporting Goods

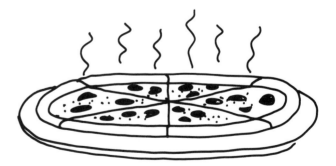

GIVING INFORMATION

Objective:

The student will provide appropriate and accurate information to a caller.

Discussion:

Teacher: When you pick up the phone after it rings, what happens next? (say "hello") Then what? (find out what the person wants) What are some reasons why people call you or your home? (talk to someone, ask a question, etc.) Usually people call with a specific reason; they want to know something or tell something. If someone wants to know something, how can you help that person? (tell them what they want to know) How much should you tell a stranger? Would you tell them that you are home alone? Why? Is there a polite way to give information? What words could you use? (please)

Worksheet I-14 This worksheet shows students giving out information over the phone. One student in each situation is doing a much better job than the other. Circle the student who is giving information appropriately. Then we will discuss your answers.

Answers:

1. B	4. B	7. A
2. A	5. B	
3. A	6. B	

Extension Activities:

1. **It's for You.** Have students monitor the number of calls to their home after school and the purpose of the call. Compare responses. Try to conclude what types of information are most commonly requested.

2. **Service with a Smile.** Have students practice giving information in a polite versus offhand or surly manner. Discuss the importance of a friendly telephone voice. (good impression)

GIVING INFORMATION

These students have just answered the phone. Someone wants some information. Circle the letter of student who you think is giving the best information to help the caller.

1. Hello, I want to speak to your father, please.

   What do you want to know? Am I in trouble?

   I'll get him. Just a minute, please.

2. What time will your sister be home?

   She'll be home in about an hour.

   Beats me.

3. Is this the Johnson home?

   Yes, it is.

   Why do you want to know?

4. Is this the Smith home?

   Boy, do you have a wrong number.

   No, I'm sorry you must have the wrong number.

5. Would you like to contribute $100 to our charity?

   Sure, why not?

   You will have to talk to my father about that.

6. Good morning! I am selling magazines. Would your like to hear about them?

   I hate to read.

   You should probably talk to my parents. They will be home at five o'clock.

7. Could I please speak to your mother?

   I'm sorry, she's not available right now. Could you call back at 3:00?

   She's not here. I'm in the house all alone.

TAKING A MESSAGE

Objective:

After hearing a brief message from a (hypothetical) caller, the student will accurately state or write down the message.

Discussion:

Teacher: When someone calls your home for a parent or brother or sister and they aren't home, what usually happens? Do your parents get mad when they find out you forgot to tell them that someone important called? Have you ever missed any important calls? How does taking a message help? A *message* is simply writing down who the caller is and what he or she wants to know. It doesn't always have to be written down, but how could that help? (less likely to forget, get mixed up) What information should you include on a message? (who called, phone number, message content)

Worksheet I-15 Here are some phone call messages that need to be written down. On the side of the paper, jot down what you think is the important part of the message. Remember to include who called, his or her phone number if necessary, and the important part of the message (not every single word).

Answers (examples):

1. Dad, Mr. Richardson will meet you at usual time.
2. Sis, Randy called and will call back.
3. Mom, call Phyllis at 877-2004.
4. Brother, Bob will call you at 9:30.
5. Aunt, watch news on CH. 10 tonight.
6. P.O. called—get package before 5.

Extension Activities:

1. **Need More Information.** Prepare similar phone messages, but omit certain pieces of information, such as the caller's name or phone number. Have students ask questions to obtain the complete message.
2. **Message Sheets.** Obtain or have students create small message pads. Discuss what information should be included. Have students use them at home and bring them in to school (if the messages aren't too personal) to discuss.

TAKING A MESSAGE

Here are some phone calls from people who want you to take a message. What could you write down so you wouldn't forget to give the message to the right person?

1. Tell your father that I will meet him at the usual time. My name is Mr. Richardson. Thank you. Good-bye.

2. This is Randy. I'll call your sister later.

3. Have your mother call me at 877-2004. My name is Phyllis.

4. I'm Bob. I don't have a phone, but I will call your brother back at nine-thirty.

5. Tell your aunt to be sure to watch the news tonight on channel 10.

6. This is the post office. You have a package to pick up before 5 o'clock.

MAKING EMERGENCY PHONE CALLS

Objective:

The student will identify what information should be relayed in an emergency situation.

Discussion:

Teacher: Remember we talked about emergency situations? What are some examples? (fire, accident, poisoning) Instead of calling the operator, who could you call for specific help with emergencies? (fire department, police department, poison control) Many cities use 911 for emergencies. What would happen if we dialed that number? (talk to an operator who would direct your call to the proper source) What would you tell the person you talk to about the emergency? What would they need to know? (who you are, your problem, address, phone number)

Worksheet I-16 This shows some examples of emergency calls. The caller got through to someone, but look at the messages. Something is missing from each one. Before the caller can get help, more information is needed. Supply the information needed on the line next to each situation. In some examples, several parts are missing.

Answers:

1. Complete name, where, phone
2. Phone
3. Phone
4. Where, phone
5. Name, where, phone
6. Name, what, where, phone

Extension Activities

1. **Help!** Compile emergency situations and randomly distribute them to students. Have students work in partners to practice giving complete information to relay to someone for help.

2. **Emergency Helpers.** If possible, have a police officer or emergency medical technician (EMT) visit your class and discuss why giving correct information over the phone is important. Ask them to relate some incidents in which a phone call and good message saved someone's life.

I–16

MAKING EMERGENCY PHONE CALLS

These students are calling for help in an emergency. But there is a problem. What is missing from each of the phone calls? Write what information is needed on the line next to each situation.

WHAT   WHERE   PHONE

1. Help, help, help! I think the house is on fire! Get over here right away! My name is Sally and I'm scared!   _____

2. My name is Eric Smith, I live at 201 North Street, and I think there is a car accident in front of my house.   _____

3. Is this the police? There is a growling dog running around the neighborhood. My name is Jane Blayne, and I live at 300 W. Apple Grove.   _____

4. I need to talk to someone at the hospital! My grandmother fell down and I think she's hurt. My name is Juan Ricardo. Hurry!   _____

5. Doctor? My little sister swallowed something and she's turning green. What should I do?   _____

6. Fire department? Help!   _____

USING A PAY PHONE

Objective:

The student will identify the correct sequence of steps necessary to operate a pay telephone.

Discussion:

Teacher: Most times you can make a phone call from a house or an office, as you can at school. But what could you do if you were on the street and needed to make a phone call? (pay phone) What do you need to make a pay phone work? (money, change) What happens after you put your money in? (dial tone) If the person you want to talk to isn't home, what happens to the money? (comes back) If the line is busy, what happens to the money? (comes back) If the person is there, what happens to the money? (stays in the phone) How much does it cost to make a phone call from a pay phone? (depends on where you live, 20 cents or 25 cents)

Worksheet I-17 There are six main steps involved in making a phone call from a pay phone. On this sheet, put them in the correct order. Then we will discuss your answers.

Answers:

    5—1—3—6—2—4

Extension Activities:

1. **Pay Phone Prowl.** Have students go on a brief walk in your downtown community area, if possible. Count how many public phones they see and note where they are located. Why are there phones in gas stations and restaurants? Discuss who might use them.

2. **Pay Phone Practice.** If possible, have students bring in correct change and make a supervised phone call from a pay phone.

USING A PAY PHONE

Here are the steps involved in using a pay phone, but they are all mixed up. Put them in order by numbering the first step with a "1," the next step with a "2," and so on.

_____   Talk to the person or get no answer or busy signal.

_____   Pick up the receiver on the phone.

_____   Listen for the dial tone on the phone.

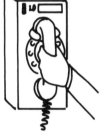

_____   Hang up.

_____   Put the correct change into the phone.

_____   Dial the number.

LEAVING A MESSAGE ON AN ANSWERING MACHINE

Objective:

The student will appropriately give information to an answering machine after making a phone call to a number.

Discussion:

Teacher: Many people aren't home during the day and miss some important phone calls. Or some people are gone a lot and don't have anyone at home to take messages. What do those people do? (get an answering machine) How does an answering machine work? (has recorded message, lets people record a message) What does the answering machine tell the caller? (probably who he has reached, what kind of message to leave) What should the caller do if he wants to leave a message? (talk after the beep) What should the caller say in the message? (brief point—not long conversation)

Worksheet I-18 Here are some answering machine messages to you, the caller. How would you respond to them? Write your answer on the cartoon next to the answering machine.

Answers (examples):

1. Hi, this is (name) and my number is (number).
2. I'm (name), today is (date), it's (time). Call me!
3. This is (name). I need to know what time you're coming over.
4. My name is (name). I'm calling for (name), and I wanted to let you know that (message).

Extension Activities:

1. **Recorded Conversations.** If you have an answering machine or know of someone who does and who wouldn't mind participating in this activity, have students call and listen to the recording. If possible, have them leave a message.

2. **Funny Recordings.** Some people are quite creative in their recorded messages. Locate some and tape them for the students. You may wish to have students use a tape recorder and design their own recorded answering message.

Name _____ Date _____

I-18

LEAVING A MESSAGE ON AN
ANSWERING MACHINE

These are some recordings from an answering machine. How would you answer them? Write what you would say in the balloon next to each machine.

1. Good morning! I'm not here to answer the phone, but I'd like to know who called. Leave your name and phone number after the beep and I'll call you back.

2. Hello, you have reached the Smith house. Please leave your name, the date and time that you called, and I'll call you back when we return.

3. This is 874-3261. We're not able to answer your call right now, but leave your name and a short message. Thank you.

4. Hello! I'm sorry we can't come to the phone right now, but we'll be happy to call you back later. Tell us who you are, who you want to talk to, and leave a message. Bye!

43

USING THE TELEPHONE DIRECTORY: WHITE PAGES

Objective:

The student will identify phone numbers located in the White Pages of the directory and locate important personal numbers.

Discussion:

Teacher: If I wanted to call each of you tonight after school, would I have to memorize all those phone numbers? Why would that be difficult? (so many) What would I have to do to find your numbers? (look in school directory, telephone book) What could I use to look up numbers of people I may not know very well? (phone book) Are the numbers just scattered around in the book? How are they organized? (alphabetically) Why? (easier to find, systematic) How many of you know if your phone number is in the phone book? How would you go about finding it? Are there only families listed in the phone book? (no) What other numbers are in there? (schools, businesses, services) In general, though, the White Pages is a list of people in a community, their phone numbers, and addresses.

Worksheet I-19 (Decide ahead of time on eight names that have some meaning or interest to the students, for example, names of other teachers, the mayor, a local celebrity, people in the class, etc.) Today I am going to have to work on finding the phone numbers and/or addresses of several people. You will have to use the phone book to find this information. Remember to use letters at the top to help you know where to start looking. (You may wish to have students work in pairs or use a small portion of the phone book and Xerox a few consecutive pages to make this more manageable.)

Answers:

(prepare an answer key ahead of time, using the names you selected)

Extension Activities:

1. **White Pages Races.** Obtain multiple copies of the local phone book of whatever source you are using. Divide students into two teams and have students race against each other (two at a time) to locate the name you call out.

2. **White Pages Addresses.** Students will realize that not only phone numbers but addresses are also printed in the phone book. Have students identify two or three neighbors who live on the same street or same apartment complex and look them up in the phone book. They should find that the same street is listed for the neighbors.

Name _____   Date _____

I–19

USING THE TELEPHONE DIRECTORY: WHITE PAGES

Your teacher will help you identify several names to look up in the phone book. Find the name; then write down the phone number, address, or page where it is found in the phone book.

	Phone Number	Address	Page
Name 1			
Name 2			
Name 3			
Name 4			
Name 5			
Name 6			
Name 7			
Name 8			

I-B TELEPHONE SKILLS   *LESSON 20*

USING THE TELEPHONE DIRECTORY: YELLOW PAGES

Objective:

When asked to find a general service or business, the student will correctly locate and identify an advertiser in the Yellow Pages to fit the description.

Discussion:

Teacher: There is another part of our phone book that we need to look at besides the White Pages. What is it? (Yellow Pages) What kind of information is included there? (business) The Yellow Pages book contains numbers and information about businesses in town. But companies are not arranged in alphabetical order by the name of the business at first; they are arranged according to the type of business they are in. Who can give me some examples of businesses in town? (list on board) If I would want to know of all the service stations, for example, what would be included? (list several local stations) If I wanted to know of places where I could buy a refrigerator, what places of business might be included? (list several) To use the Yellow Pages, you first have to decide what you are looking for, and then use the Yellow Pages to find all your choices. Remember, after you have your key word, you can use alphabetical order to find the names of different businesses.

Worksheet I-20 Here are situations in which someone needs to use the Yellow Pages. The first thing is to find the key word so you will know where to look up the companies in that business. For the examples on the worksheet, circle the best answer.

Answers:

1. Jewelry		5. Pet shops	
2. Motels		6. Churches	
3. Restaurants		7. Dentists	
4. Refrigerators		8. Music stores	

Extension Activities:

1. **Give Me a Name.** For each situation on the worksheet, have students use the Yellow Pages to look up the key word and find at least one business that could help with that service.

2. **Christmas List.** Have students make an early Christmas list of items that they would like to obtain. Then decide on a key word (toys, bicycles, camping equipment) for each item and proceed to have the student look up businesses in the Yellow Pages that could supply that item.

USING THE TELEPHONE DIRECTORY: YELLOW PAGES

To use the Yellow Pages, think of the best word or two that would help you find the business or service you need. Read each of the situations below, and decide which words would best help each person find the business that they need. Circle your answer.

1. Mrs. Smith wants a new diamond necklace. She wants to know where to look for one.

   printers   jewelry   photographers

2. Mr. Riley is staying overnight in another city. He needs to find a place to stay.

   laundry   mobile homes   motels

3. John and Marcia want to go out to eat for a special occasion.

   restaurants   florists   radio stations

4. Max has a broken refrigerator and needs to get it fixed.

   refrigerators   pizza   firewood

5. Sally would like a new puppy for a pet.

   zoos   pet shops   schools

6. The Robinson family just moved to town and is looking for a church close by.

   hotels   childcare   churches

7. Ben broke a tooth playing hockey outside and needs to see a dentist.

   doctors   bowling   dentists

8. Peter wants to get new strings for his guitar.

   lawn mowers   music stores   locksmiths

Dear Parents,

Our next group of lessons centers on money—counting it, using it, and saving it. If your child does not get an allowance, this may be a good time to talk about jobs he can do around the house in return for some spending money. On the other hand, earning some "saving money" is not a bad idea, either! Your child is old enough to accompany you to the bank to open a savings account for himself or herself. It is very motivating (for all of us) to set a goal and then save up the money to finally go out and get it! Whether it's a skateboard or designer jeans, a goal of saving up enough money to get something you really want is a great incentive to learn about saving.

Also consider letting your child help you count your change, hand you the correct coins from time to time, and see if you have enough money to get him or her a candy bar or other treat. Certainly it's easier for you to do it yourself, but an excellent opportunity for your child to practice real-life money situations.

Happy counting!

Sincerely,

_____

Teacher

Skill Sheet #3: Progress Report

+ mastered
√ emerging
− not mastered

Student name	Coins/bills	Counting	Value	Safe place	Savings	Earning	Spending	Comments

COINS AND BILLS

Objective:

Given examples of real and printed coins/bills, the student will identify the coin/bill.

Discussion:

Teacher: I saw something at the store that I really wanted to buy. What would I need to get it? (money, charge card) Why do people use money? (to buy things) *Money* is something used for payment, to buy something. Who knows what the different kinds of money in our country are? I'll give you a hint—one is a dime. Can you think of others? (penny, quarter, nickel, half dollar) A piece of metal money is called a *coin.* Paper money is called a *bill.* Can anyone think of the kinds of bills that we have? (one dollar bill, five dollar bill, etc.)

Worksheet I-21 On this worksheet, you are going to practice looking at coins and bills and figuring out what they are. Here you will only have to match the coins and bills with the names of them. Then we will do some other activities with money. Write the letter next to the coins on the worksheet.

Answers:

1.	f	6.	b
2.	c	7.	i
3.	j	8.	a
4.	g	9.	d
5.	h	10.	e

Extension Activities:

1. **Coin Flash Cards.** Have students make series of flash cards bearing a coin print on one side and the name on the other side. Pair students with a partner and have races in which the object is to identify the coins (10–15) in a stack without missing any.

2. **I'm Thinking Of.** Allow students to handle and observe actual coins (and bills, if desired). Have them think how they can remember which coin is which. Students find all sorts of cues to help them (the direction the person is facing, Jefferson's ponytail, the color of the coin, the ridged edge of the dime and quarter, etc.) Then have students take turns giving clues as to which coin they are thinking of.

COINS AND BILLS

Match the groups of coins and bills on the left with the description on the right. Write the letter of your choice on the line after the coins and bills.

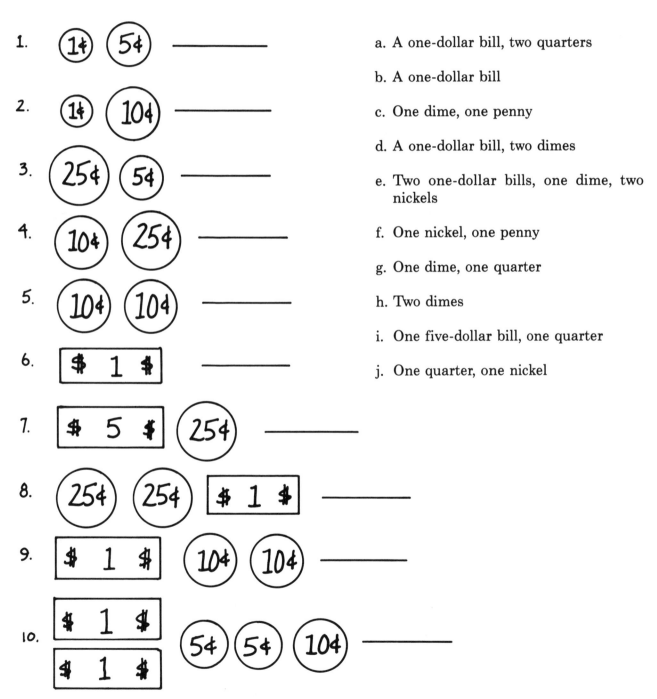

1. 1¢ 5¢ _____

2. 1¢ 10¢ _____

3. 25¢ 5¢ _____

4. 10¢ 25¢ _____

5. 10¢ 10¢ _____

6. $ 1 $ _____

7. $ 5 $ 25¢ _____

8. 25¢ 25¢ $ 1 $ _____

9. $ 1 $ 10¢ 10¢ _____

10. $ 1 $ $ 1 $ 5¢ 5¢ 10¢ _____

a. A one-dollar bill, two quarters

b. A one-dollar bill

c. One dime, one penny

d. A one-dollar bill, two dimes

e. Two one-dollar bills, one dime, two nickels

f. One nickel, one penny

g. One dime, one quarter

h. Two dimes

i. One five-dollar bill, one quarter

j. One quarter, one nickel

COUNTING COINS

Objective:

Given amounts of coins, the student will correctly count out the total amount.

Discussion:

Teacher: Let's see what you know about counting money. If I wanted to have 10 cents, what are some ways I could get that using coins? (one dime, two nickels, one nickel and five pennies, ten pennies) What about 20 cents? Or 30 cents? You see, there are lots of ways I can get the amount I need. What if I gave you two nickels and three pennies? What would that amount be? (13 cents) How did you figure that out? If I gave you one quarter and one nickel, what would that be? (30 cents)

Worksheet I-22 On this sheet, you are going to practice counting the amount of money you have in coins. Remember to put the cents sign after your amount, because all of these are less than one dollar, so we call them cents. Some of you have probably figured out shortcuts to counting coins, so we'll have you tell us your secrets when we discuss the answers.

Answers:

1. 12 cents	6. 37 cents
2. 30 cents	7. 46 cents
3. 27 cents	8. 40 cents
4. 41 cents	9. 35 cents
5. 60 cents	10. 51 cents

Extension Activities:

1. **Counting Relays.** Divide into several teams and distribute coins to each. Call out an amount (under one dollar) or write it on the board. When you say "Go," a designated player from each team will use the coins to count out the amount. First one wins a point for their team. Then change amounts and change players.

2. **Handful of Coins.** Again using teams, place various coins into jars or cups. Players from each team pick four coins randomly from their cup. The player with the highest value (four quarters would be the most) wins a point. Then mix the coins up and repeat with the next player.

COUNTING COINS

Here are some groups of coins. Count the value of each group and write the amount in cents on the line next to each group.

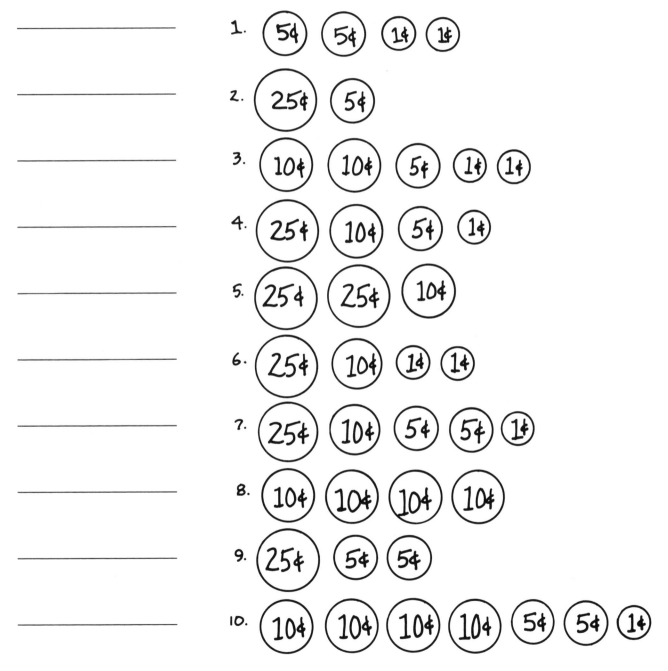

1. (5¢) (5¢) (1¢) (1¢)

2. (25¢) (5¢)

3. (10¢) (10¢) (5¢) (1¢) (1¢)

4. (25¢) (10¢) (5¢) (1¢)

5. (25¢) (25¢) (10¢)

6. (25¢) (10¢) (1¢) (1¢)

7. (25¢) (10¢) (5¢) (5¢) (1¢)

8. (10¢) (10¢) (10¢) (10¢)

9. (25¢) (5¢) (5¢)

10. (10¢) (10¢) (10¢) (10¢) (5¢) (5¢) (1¢)

RECOGNIZING VALUE OF ITEMS

Objective:

Given an item or picture of an item, the student will estimate the item's approximate value in terms of dollars or cents.

Discussion:

Teacher: If you had $100, could you buy a ruler from the office? Could you buy a brand new car? What could you buy with only $1? What can you buy for a dime? Why do some things cost more than others? (bigger, better) How much do you think a pair of new jeans costs? What about a pencil? How do we know how much to pay for things? (familiar with the items, advertising)

Worksheet I-23 Today you are going to be a detective. Your job is to find out how much these items cost. You can use pretty much any helpful source. Some examples are the newspaper, magazines, or going to a store. When we're all done, let's compare findings and see who found the cheapest and most expensive items. Write down where you found the cost. That can affect the price.

Answers:

(will vary according to your area)

Extension Activities

1. **Ordering the Items.** Once you have established a median or average price, have students list the items in order from least expensive to most expensive. It may take them more than one try.

2. **If I Had $100.** Tell each student that they have just been given $100. They must spend all of it, without going over the amount. They must also have at least five items on their list. See what they come up with! They must list the item, the price, and the total spent. (It's harder than it seems!)

RECOGNIZING VALUE OF ITEMS

Find out about how much the following items cost. You can use magazines and newspapers, real stores, or other people to help you. Compare your answers with those of other people.

HOW MUCH IS . . .	Price	Where I Found It

1. A sports car

2. A banana

3. A T-shirt

4. A paperback book

5. A pencil

6. A candy bar

7. A bar of soap

8. A half gallon of ice cream

9. A living room couch

10. A cocker spaniel

KEEPING MONEY IN A SAFE PLACE

Objective:

The student will identify places where money can be kept safely.

Discussion:

Teacher: If I had some change, where would I most likely keep it? (purse, pocket, wallet) Why wouldn't I keep it in my hand? (hard to hold) Why not in a pocket with a hole? (lose it) If I had a lot of money, where would be a safe place to keep it? (bank) Why would keeping money in a place like a bank be safer than just letting it lay around the house? Don't people rob banks? (still fairly safe, insurance) How do I know I can get my money back if I leave it in a bank? (bank book, checking account) Name some other safe places to keep money.

Worksheet I-24 Here are some examples of students who keep their money in various places. Decide which places you think are safe and which are not. Then we'll discuss why you picked certain ones as safe. Write *safe* or *not safe* on the line.

Answers:

1. Not safe
2. Safe
3. Not safe (probably)
4. Not safe
5. Safe
6. Safe
7. Not safe (probably)
8. Safe
9. Safe
10. Safe

Extension Activities:

1. **Token Economy.** For fun and experience, try using chips or paper money from construction paper to "pay" students for various activities at school. See what they do with the tokens they have accumulated. Some will probably be careless; others will devise elaborate means to safeguard their loot!

2. **Bank Search.** Using the Yellow Pages or other community resources, have students list all the banks in the community. This could also include savings and loans or any other institutions that provide a savings service for customers.

Name _____   Date _____

I–24

KEEPING MONEY IN A SAFE PLACE

These students have some money. Some of them are keeping their money in safe places; others are not. Write *safe* or *not safe* after each example.

1. Frank keeps his money in his desk at school. _____

2. Susan got a dollar from her dad. She put it in her piggy bank in her room. _____

3. Amy is using her five-dollar bill as a book-mark in her library book. _____

4. Ben keeps his milk money in his back pocket with a hole in it. _____

5. Sharon has a coin purse inside her larger purse for her coins. _____

6. Darla keeps her money in a savings account at the local bank. _____

7. Steve gives his money to his little brother to keep for him. _____

8. Joy keeps her change in a wallet. _____

9. Rick gives his money to his mother to keep for him in her bank account. _____

10. Ramon has a small safe with a padlock for his money. _____

SAVINGS ACCOUNT

Objective:

The student will explain how a savings account works to give the customer interest on his money.

Discussion:

Teacher: If I borrowed some money from you, let's say $10, how much do you think I should pay you back? Does anyone think I should pay back more than $10? Why or why not? (pay for the privilege of using the money) We talked about a bank being a safe place to keep money. One way is to open a *savings account.* That's a special record of the money that you put into the bank. But there's another reason why a savings account is good for you. Does anyone know why? (interest) The bank will pay you *interest* for letting them keep and "borrow" your money. Interest is extra money for the customer, depending on how much you have in your savings account.

Worksheet I-25 Sara is an imaginary student who wants to save $100 before Christmas. This worksheet tells some of the things that happen to her and her money, including being paid interest on the money she keeps in her savings account. Work through each problem and see if you can figure out how much she saved before Christmas.

Answers:

1.	$25	5.	$81
2.	$37	6.	$86
3.	$39	7.	$96
4.	$51	8.	$102

Extension Activities:

1. **Interest Rates.** Have students look through local newspaper bank ads to find out what they are paying for interest on savings accounts. Discuss what this means (simply) and show how a single percentage point makes a difference.

2. **Interest on Token Economy.** If you started a token economy, begin paying "interest" on the amount that students have saved. Set up a fixed payment schedule, such as every Friday, for the interest to be paid out to students.

I–25

SAVINGS ACCOUNT

Sara the Student opened a savings account at her local bank. Solve the problems below in order and see if you can figure out how much money she has saved before Christmas. Did she reach her goal of $100?

1. Sara's aunt gave her $25 for her birthday. She put it immediately in a savings account. What's her total?

   _____

2. A few days later, she got $5 from her uncle in Chicago and $7 from her cousin in the next state. How much does she have now?

   _____

3. Sara got a note from the bank that said she had earned $2 in interest. How much money is in her savings account now?

   _____

4. Sara did some babysitting for her little cousin next door and earned $2 an hour. She worked for 6 hours. She put all of it into her savings account. How big is the account now?

   _____

5. Later, Sara sold her bicycle for $35. She spent $5 on candy and a book, but the rest went into the savings account. How much is in the account now?

   _____

6. A bank note came for Sara, telling her that she had earned $5 on her savings account that month. Now how much does she have?

   _____

7. Sara's dad told her that if she had saved at least $75 by now, he would give her $10. What do you think happened?

   _____

8. Sara's money earned another $6 in interest. If this is the last payment before Christmas, did Sara reach her goal of $100?

   _____

EARNING MONEY

Objective:

The student will list at least three ways that an adult can earn money and three ways that a student can earn money.

Discussion:

Teacher: Suppose I wanted to open a savings account and earn some interest on the money to save up for something. First, I would have to get some money. How do people get money? (someone gives it to them, they find it, they work, they invest) Most people get their money by earning it. To *earn* money means to work for or provide a service for someone and then receive money as payment. How do people that you know earn money? Can people your age earn money too? How? Sometimes people earn money by providing a service. A *service* is something that you do for someone to help him. What are some services that you could do for people in your neighborhood? (wash car, mow lawn, rake leaves, babysit)

Worksheet I-26 Here are some services that adults or students could do to earn some money. Write down whether you think the job could be done by only an adult, or whether a student could do it. (Clarify that they should write *student* even if an adult could perform the service, but most likely a student-aged person could earn money in this capacity.)

Answers:

1.	Student	6.	Adult
2.	Adult	7.	Student
3.	Student	8.	Adult
4.	Student	9.	Student
5.	Adult	10.	Student

Extension Activities:

1. **At Your Service.** Have students page through the local Yellow Pages ads in the phone book and list at least ten services that are described. Continue the project by having students list the title of the person most likely to perform the service (e.g., car repair—mechanic, weeding—gardener)

2. **Job List.** Have students compile a list of jobs that they could potentially do to earn money. Then have specific students indicate which jobs they actually have performed. They could also estimate how much each job is worth in terms of dollars per hour. Does dog-sitting pay more than babysitting? When is the best time to have a lemonade stand?

Name _____ Date _____

I-26

EARNING MONEY

Here is a list of some services that people could do to help earn money. Write Adult if you think the service should be done by an adult. Write Student if someone your age could help with this service.

1. Mow the lawn for the people who live next door _____

2. Repair an engine in a car _____

3. Walk a dog every day after school _____

4. Babysit for the children who live in your neighborhood _____

5. Put a new roof on a two-story house _____

6. Put a cast on a broken arm _____

7. Deliver newspapers _____

8. Drive a schoolbus _____

9. Rake leaves _____

10. Sell lemonade in the summer in your front yard _____

SPENDING MONEY

Objective:

The student will identify at least three appropriate items or ways that he or she could spend a designated amount of money.

Discussion:

Teacher: After I have saved money for a while, I may decide that I wish to spend it. What are some things I could spend my money on? (vacation, clothes) What do you think I should consider before I spend my hard-earned money? (what I really want, my overall needs, how much I have, etc.) Let's make a list. (include *have, need, want*)

Worksheet I-27 Today you are going to give advice to five students who are thinking about spending some money. Read each situation and think about what you would advise each of them. There is no real right or wrong answer, but be able to tell me why you picked *yes* or *no* for each situation.

Answers: (examples)

1. No—can't buy a car for $15
2. Yes—he'd enjoy the purchase
3. Yes—if she doesn't have too many other people to buy for
4. No—he should get the bike repaired first
5. Yes—she really loves the cat

Extension Activities:

1. **Where My Money Went.** Have students keep track of how much money they spend in a typical week, what their purchases are, and what the largest expense is. Compare answers. Do girls spend more than boys?

2. **Comparison Shopping.** Have students research the price of a certain item (popular record or cassette, name-brand jeans or shoes, etc.) at several stores around town. Which places will give them the most for their money?

I–27

SPENDING MONEY

These students want to spend some money. Keep in mind how much each has to spend, how great the student's need is, and how badly the student wants the item. Decide whether or not you think the student should spend the money. Circle Yes or No next to each situation.

Why/Why Not?

1. Juan has $15. He is thinking about buying a new car. He would like a car, but he would also like other things more. Should he spend his money on a car?

   Yes   No

   _____

   _____

   _____

2. Randy has $20. He is crazy about computers and knows that there is a sale at the store. Do you think he should spend his money on a computer disk?

   Yes   No

   _____

   _____

   _____

3. It's almost Christmas. Jenny would like to buy her mom a bottle of perfume for $10 and some stationery for $5. She knows her mom would really like the gifts. She has $50 to spend. Do you think she should do this?

   Yes   No

   _____

   _____

   _____

4. Bobby has $30. He wants to buy a new football for $25, but he also wants to get his bike tire repaired for $10. He can't do both right now. Do you think he should get the football?

   Yes   No

   _____

   _____

5. Amy has $60. Her cat needs to have an operation that will cost $50. Amy can give the cat away to a neighbor who will take care of it, or she can take it to the vet for the operation. Amy loves the cat. Should Amy spend the money on the cat?

   Yes   No

   _____

   _____

   _____

PARENT LETTER #4   TIME CONCEPTS

© 1992 by The Center for Applied Research in Education

Dear Parents,

The activities covered in the next unit involve basic time concepts, such as awareness of the days of the week and months of the year, planning ahead for events, and becoming familiar with measuring time by using a clock and calendar.

You can help your child at home in the following ways:

- Post a monthly calendar in the kitchen. Each morning before school, check off the day and note any appointments written on the paper.

- Purchase an inexpensive watch (digital is fine) for your child to wear. Ask him or her often to tell you the time.

- As daily events occur (getting up, getting ready to go to school, anticipating dinner, watching television), have your child locate and tell you the time. Help him or her pair up significant daily events with the time they occur.

- On a yearly calendar, mark all the significant family events such as birthdays, anniversaries, vacations, holidays, and so on. Have your child take special note of what is going to happen each month.

- Take pictures of your child and display them in a prominent place. Show that time changes him or her also, and note changes in height, weight, and appearance.

- As you and your child do things outside, take particular note of the signs of each season. Discuss what will happen next as you approach the next season.

Time passes so quickly—enjoy the time that you can spend with your child!

Sincerely,

_____

Teacher

I-D TIME CONCEPTS

Skill Sheet #4: Progress Report

+ mastered
√ emerging
− not mastered

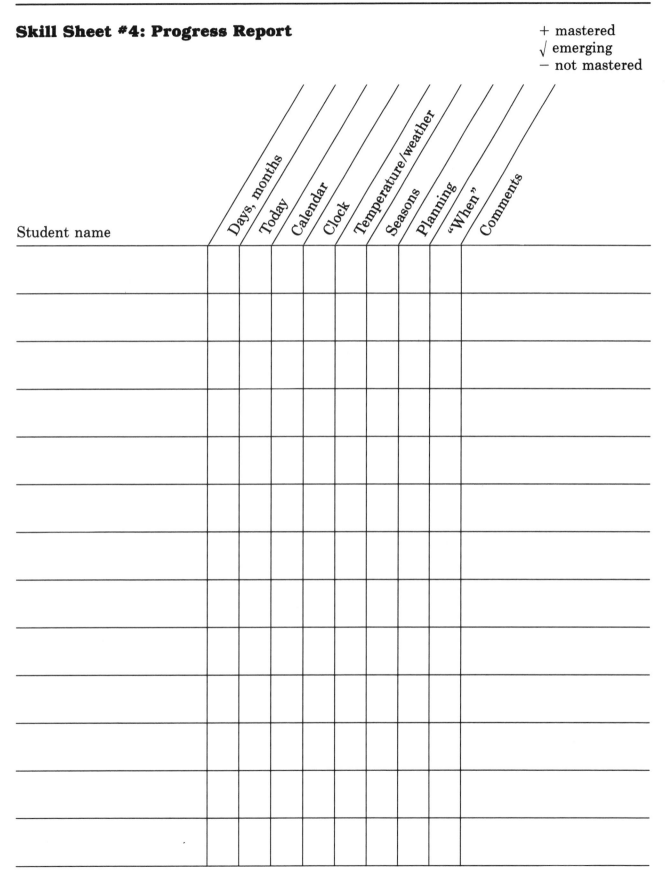

Student name	Days, months	Today	Calendar	Clock	Temperature/weather	Seasons	Planning	"When"	Comments

DAYS AND MONTHS

Objective:

Upon request, the student will state the days of the week and months of the year in chronological order.

Discussion:

Teacher: How did you know to come to school today? Why didn't you come on Sunday? If it were the middle of July, would you be in school? (if summer school) If it were Wednesday today, would it be a long time until the weekend? What if it were January? Would it be a long time until Halloween? Help! We need to get the days and months organized! When I ask you to tell me the days of the week, I want you to say, "Monday, Tuesday, Wednesday, Thursday, Friday, Saturday, Sunday." When I ask you to tell me the months of the year, I want you to say, "January, February, March, April, May, June, July, August, September, October, November, December."

Worksheet I-28 These students are playing a game that we will play in our class later. Each has a tag with a day or month named on it. Put the students in order by numbering the boxes below them 1 to 7 or 1 to 12.

Answers:

6-2-5-1-4-3-7
5-8-1-3-9-12   and   4-2-11-7-6-10

Extension Activities:

1. **Relays.** Assign students name cards with days/months, similar to the worksheet. Tell them that when you say "go" they must find their place in a lineup. Time them on their trials to see how fast they are. Switch cards often.

2. **Before and After.** Using the same cards, alter the strategy by having students tell the day/month preceding and following their day/month. Toss a bean bag among the students to select who goes next. Keep the pace quick!

Name _____   Date _____

I–28

DAYS AND MONTHS

The students on the top part of the page are playing the Days of the Week Game. The students on the bottom are playing the Months of the Year Game. Both groups want to get the players in the right order. Number each group (1–7 and 1–12) in the correct order.

67

TODAY

Objective:

The student will be able to relate the present day, month, number, and year.

Discussion:

Teacher: What day is it today? How did you know? If I asked you what the *date* is today, what would you say? How is the *day* different from the *date?* (one is the name of the day of the week; other is three parts—month, number, year) What was the date five days ago? When I ask you for the *day,* tell me the word that ends with—day. When I ask you for the *date,* tell me the three parts: the month first, then the number, then the year.

Worksheet I-29 On this worksheet the teacher is asking students to tell her the day or the date. You are to circle the student in each group who is giving her the correct answer. You don't have to know which day or date is the actual one, because we don't know when the stories happened. But look for all parts of the information needed in each situation. Don't worry about what the actual months or days are. We'll do that for real very soon.

Answers:

1. Second	5. Second
2. First	6. Second
3. Second	7. First
4. Second	8. Second

Extension Activities:

1. **What's Today?** Each day, preferably in the morning, have students recite the day and date. At frequent times during the day, question students as to the current date.

2. **Find a Date.** Have students be on the lookout for places in which a date is used, for example, library due dates, newspaper, and future doctor's appointments. You may want to introduce using numbers to indicate months (as in 10/16/53 for October 16, 1953).

Name _____   Date _____

I–29

TODAY

The teacher is asking the students questions about the *day* and the *date*. Circle the student in each situation who is answering correctly.

USING A CALENDAR

Objective:

Given a specific day and/or date, the student will use a calendar to locate the requested information.

Discussion:

Teacher: Who can tell me what the day is today? Who can tell me today's date? How did you know? (heard someone, looked at paper or calendar) Does anyone know what an orderly arrangement of days is called? It's a *calendar.* It's a way of showing how all of the days go together to make up months and a year. Remember how many months in a year there are? (12) Usually a calendar shows all of the days in one year. There are 365 days, and usually a calendar shows one month at a time.

Worksheet I-30 Use the calendar on the second worksheet to help you answer the questions on the first page. Write your answers on the line following each question.

Answers:

1. July	6. Monday	11. June
2. 31	7. 5	12. August
3. 1990	8. 9	13. July 17, 1990
4. July 4, 1990	9. 4	14. July 26, 1990
5. Friday	10. 5	15. July 19, 1990

Extension Activities:

1. **Calendar Puzzle.** Hand out old calendars (monthly sheets may work best at first) cut into jigsawlike shapes. Have students put the calendar together. Ask what clues they used to help them. (numbers, days of week, etc.)

2. **Questions by Students.** Hand out calendar sheets to students and have each write five questions similar to the ones on the worksheet. Exchange calendars and questions. How accurate were the questions? (students should also provide an answer key)

I–30

USING A CALENDAR

The following worksheet shows a month from a calendar. Use it to answer the following questions. Write your answer on the line next to each question.

1. What month is it on the calendar?   _____

2. How many days are in the month?   _____

3. What year is it on the calendar?   _____

4. What day of the week is Independence Day on?   _____

5. What day of the week is #27?   _____

6. What day of the week is #16?   _____

7. What is the number of the first Thursday?   _____

8. What is the number of the second Monday?   _____

9. How many Wednesdays are in this month?   _____

10. How many Tuesdays are in this month?   _____

11. What month came before this one?   _____

12. What month comes after this one?   _____

13. What is the date of the day with the *?   _____

14. What is the date of the day with the $?   _____

15. What is the date after July 18, 1990?   _____

© 1992 by The Center for Applied Research in Education

JULY, 1990

SUNDAY	MONDAY	TUESDAY	WEDNESDAY	THURSDAY	FRIDAY	SATURDAY
1	2	3	4 Independence Day	5	6	7
8	9	10	11	12	13	14
15	16	17 ✳	18	19	20	21
22	23	24	25	26 $	27	28
29	30	31			JUNE S M T W T F S 1 2 3 4 5 6 7 8 9 10 11 12 13 14 15 16 17 18 19 20 21 22 23 24 25 26 27 28 29 30	AUGUST S M T W T F S 1 2 3 4 5 6 7 8 9 10 11 12 13 14 15 16 17 18 19 20 21 22 23 24 25 26 27 28 29 30 31

USING A CLOCK

Objective:

Given a clock (traditional face or digital), the student will identify the correct time.

Discussion:

Teacher: It's (state present time). How did I know that? (looked at watch, clock) Why is it important to know what time it is? (don't miss appointments, stay on task) What time do you get up in the morning? What time is school over? What's on television at 8:00 tonight? What are some other important times for you?

Worksheet I-31 Here is a list of some events that are going to happen. On the right side are clocks that show the time. Circle the clock that shows the correct time that the event will happen.

Answers:

1.	First clock	6.	First clock
2.	First clock	7.	Second clock
3.	First clock	8.	Second clock
4.	Second clock	9.	First clock
5.	Second clock	10.	Second clock

Extension Activities:

1. **What Was That Time?** Have students use the worksheet to practice reading the times on the clocks that were the incorrect times for the event listed. You may also wish to make flash cards of clocks set at various times with the correct time written on the back.

2. **My Time Card.** Have students list various important events that occur in their lives, such as bus times, sports events times, television programming, and so on. Using a blank clock face, have students draw hands on the clock to indicate their important times.

USING A CLOCK

Match the events on the left with the correct clock on the right. Circle the clock that shows the correct time.

1. You want to watch a football game on television that starts at 8:30.

2. The bus is coming to pick you up at 7:25.

3. Your best friend is coming over at 4:15.

4. Your mother is going to call you from her office at 3:30.

5. You are supposed to pick up your sister from the babysitter's house at 5:05.

6. Your dog has an appointment at the vet at 6:00.

7. You are supposed to be home for dinner at 5:45.

8. If you leave home at 7:35, you will get to school on time.

9. Your friends are meeting you at the hamburger place at 4:30. Don't be late!

10. Your library book is due today, and it closes at 1:00. Plan ahead!

TEMPERATURE AND WEATHER

Objective:

Using a thermometer, weather forecast, or observation, the student will describe temperature and weather conditions.

Discussion:

Teacher: If I said, "It must be 100 degrees outside!" how would it feel? (hot) If I said, "Take your umbrella," what do you think the weather might be like? (rainy) What clues do we have to know what it's like outside? (thermometer, et cetera) A *thermometer* is a helpful instrument that lets us know how hot or cold it feels. The *temperature* is a number that we know is hot, cold or somewhere in between. If a thermometer told us that the temperature was 25 degrees, would that feel hot, cold, or in between? (probably cold) Look outside. How would you describe the weather? (sunny, rainy, cloudy) *Weather* means what it is like outside in terms of heat, dryness, and clouds.

Worksheet I-32 The temperature and weather conditions have a lot to do with what we do sometimes. In the situations on this worksheet, the temperature and weather forecast is given. Decide whether or not the activity planned is a good one for that day, and answer the questions about the activity on the lines.

Answers:

Situation 1—1. Summer clothes; 2. No; 3. Yes
Situation 2—1. No; 2. only on face; 3. maybe an hour
Situation 3—1. Warm winter clothes; 2. no; 3. extremely short (if at all)

Extension Activities:

1. **Watch the Weather.** Collect weather predictions for several weeks and use them to make a weather chart for the month. Discuss questions such as how accurate were the predictions? Are there patterns or trends to the weather/temperature?

2. **Good Activities for That Day.** Why would it be difficult to have a picnic in the snow? (there wouldn't be any ants to bother you, but the wind and ground might present some problems) Using a large thermometer poster, have students draw or collect pictures of activities that would be appropriate for that temperature range. For example, ice skating and skiing would be fun activities for lower temperatures, and swimming or picnics would be good activities for higher temperatures.

I–32

TEMPERATURE AND WEATHER

What would you wear or bring or do in the following situations? Use the temperature and weather clues to help you make your decisions. Write your answers on the lines.

Situation 1—The Picnic

Temperature: 72 degrees
Weather forecast: sunny and clear all day

1. What would you wear?_____

2. Would you bring an umbrella?_____

3. Would you bring suntan lotion?_____

Situation 2—Playing Outside

Temperature: 35 degrees
Weather forecast: sunny and clear

1. Would you wear shorts and a T-shirt today?_____

2. Would it be a good day to get a tan?_____

3. Would you stay outside for a long time?_____

Situation 3—Snowball Fight

Temperature: −5 degrees
Weather forecast: bitter winds, clouds

1. What would you wear?_____

2. Would you fly a kite today?_____

3. How long would your snowball fight be?_____

SEASONS

Objective:

The student will identify the four seasons and state characteristics of each.

Discussion:

Teacher: It's snowing outside! Just kidding—but is that likely to happen today? If you keep track of the temperature and the weather conditions for a long time, you'll find out that there are four basic patterns. These are called the *seasons.* Can anyone name all four? The seasons are spring, summer, fall, and winter. What is it like outside in the spring? How about the other seasons?

Worksheet I-33 There are certain characteristics, or patterns, for each season. Read over the list of things you might feel or do, and then write each item under the name of the season in which you might feel or do that thing.

Answers: (may vary)

Spring: May be good time for an umbrella/gets very wet/plant flowers/fly a kite/may be windy
Summer: Gets very hot/a good time for playing outside/take sunscreen/mow the lawn/good time for swimming
Fall: May be windy/rake leaves
Winter: Gets very cold/wear your mittens/have snowball fights/shovel snow

Extension Activities:

1. **Month by Month.** Have students consider each month and categorize it into a season, weather and temperature pattern, and typical events for that month (including holidays). You may want to pick a theme (e.g., Spring Fever, Winter Fun) and have students draw pictures or write stories to illustrate events specific to that season.

2. **Changing Leaves.** As the seasons change, have students change the leaves (construction paper or real, if possible) on a large cutout tree (trunk with long branches). In winter, the tree should be bare or snowcovered. Outlining a hand makes a good pattern for cutting out leaves from colored construction paper. Each student may want to contribute his or her handprint to the "class tree." (You could accessorize the tree by adding a wayward kite, a squirrel, an apple, etc.)

Name _____ Date _____

I–33

SEASONS

Below is a list of temperatures, weather conditions, and events that may occur during the seasons of the year. Your part of the country may be a little different, so you may want to change or add to this list. Write each characteristic under the name of the season.

List:

gets very hot	gets very cold	may be windy	gets very wet
a good time for playing outside	good time for swimming	good time for an umbrella	wear your mittens
wear your swimming suit	take sunscreen	rake leaves	have snowball fights
plant flowers	mow the lawn	shovel snow	fly a kite

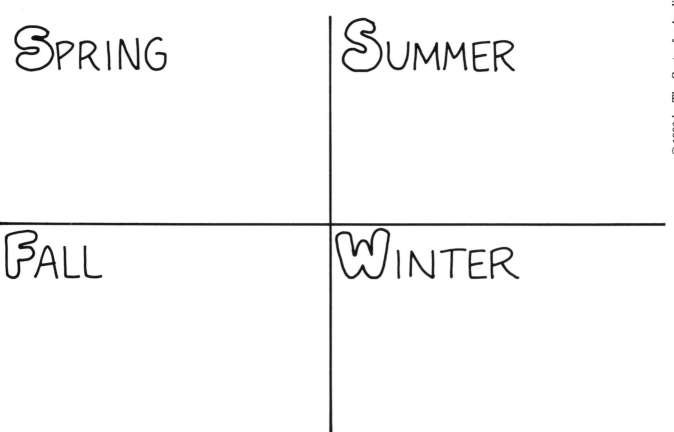

SPRING

SUMMER

FALL

WINTER

PLANNING AHEAD

Objective:

Given a calendar and real or hypothetical events, the student will anticipate and plan events in a reasonable order.

Discussion:

Teacher: Would you like to hear my list of what I'm going to do next week? On Monday, I'm going to fly to Alaska. On Tuesday, I have a dentist appointment. On Wednesday, I'm having gall bladder surgery. On Thursday, I'm meeting the president and his cabinet to talk about educational programs. Do you see a problem with this schedule? What? (transporting self around the country quickly, surgery complications) Of course, that's not my real schedule, but what if it were? Any suggestions for changing things around? (allow time, change order) When you plan events, you should keep in mind (1) how long it may take and (2) what might happen that will affect other plans.

Worksheet I-34 Sometimes you can make plans for things to happen because most of the time nothing goes wrong. These students are making plans. Help them by circling the answer that you think is the best plan for their time. Then we'll discuss what could go wrong (although it is hoped nothing will).

Answers:

1. Take the dog out
2. Saturday or Sunday
3. In winter
4. Get a haircut
5. Thursday before Sally's party
6. Friday night . . .

Extension Activities

1. **What Could Go Wrong?** In each situation on the worksheet, have students discuss what could possibly happen to make their choice unworkable. (For example, in situation #4 perhaps David would have to wait a week to get an appointment with the stylist he wants. In 5, perhaps Sally's house is so huge that they would need to start cleaning up on Monday—being careful not to mess up the house during the other days!

2. **How Long Does It Take?** Have students estimate how long certain events usually take. Examples may include going to a movie, going to the dentist, cleaning a room, doing homework, taking out the garbage, building a model, brushing teeth, and so on. Students may be surprised at how much (or how little) time is actually involved in these tasks.

PLANNING AHEAD

These students are making plans. Help them decide what to do when. Circle your answer.

1. Mandy is supposed to clean her room before her cousins come over to play. She is also to walk the dog and feed him. What should she do first.

    take the dog out   clean her room

2. Luis wants to go to the big museum for an entire day. His dad said he would be glad to go with him, but he can't go after work because there isn't enough time to see everything they want to see. When do you think they should plan to go to the museum?

    when his dad doesn't work anymore   Saturday or Sunday
    and is retired

3. Maria wants to go skiing. Sometimes the ski slopes are closed when there isn't enough snow. When do you think Maria should plan to go skiing?

    in fall   in winter

4. David wants to get a haircut and go to the ballpark with friends and go to the movies. Today was a very busy day and he only has time to get one thing done. What should he plan to do?

    see a movie   get a haircut   play ball with friends

5. Sally is having a birthday party Friday night. Sally's father is having a party Saturday night. When would be a good time to clean up the house?

    Thursday before Sally's party   Monday before Sally's party

6. Randy can have a friend stay overnight one night this week. He wants to spend as much time as he can with his friend. Which night do you think he would choose?

    Friday night with no other   Tuesday night before school
    plans for Saturday   on Wednesday

WHAT HAPPENS WHEN?

Objective:

Students will answer "time" questions appropriately and accurately by giving the day, date, time, month, year, or season.

Discussion:

Teacher: What day is it today? What's the date? What time is it? What season is it? All of these questions are about time and knowing when something happens. They are all asking about *today,* but they all were different answers. It's *Monday,* but it's also *October.* Listen for what exact question I am asking, so you will know how to answer my question. In what month is your birthday? In which season is your birthday?

Worksheet I-35 This worksheet reviews the different ways to look at time that we have talked about: the day, the date, the month, year, season, and clock time. Be sure to read each question carefully so you are answering the question. Write your answer on the line next to each situation.

Answers:

1. Will vary
2. Will vary
3. December
4. Will vary
5. Summer
6. Will vary
7. Will vary
8. Will vary

Extension Activities:

1. **On Target.** To help students conceptualize how our measurement of time can become increasingly more specific, use a target poster with several concentric circles, labeled year, season, month, day, number. Have the arrow hitting the "number" circle and change information on the target (daily for the inner circle) as the time changes.

2. **New Month Holiday.** Create a holiday for the first day of each new month. Students may wish to start a special tradition or festival (e.g., November Leaf Dance, February "Send-the-President-a-Valentine" tradition) to kick off the new month.

WHAT HAPPENS WHEN?

Each student below wants to know when something happens. Read each question carefully and write the best answer on the line next to each item.

1. Alissa — What time do you go to lunch? _____

2. Mark — What is the day after tomorrow? _____

3. Richard — What month is Christmas in? _____

4. Claudia — When is your birthday? _____

5. Max — In which season do you go sailing? _____

6. Kim — When would be a good day for us to get together to play after school? _____

7. Linda — What time do you have to go to bed? _____

8. Ben — This library book is due tomorrow. What is the date? _____

PARENT LETTER #5   BASIC READING AND WRITING SKILLS

Dear Parents,

It is extremely important today for children to be able to understand how people communicate in writing. All around us are words, signs, and directions that require some ability to read and comprehend the message.

This unit focuses on survival skills for areas of reading and writing. Your child will be working on building up a list of words which are important to him or her. Signs around us, such as traffic signs, signs which give warnings or other information, and other common words will be studied.

Writing is another skill which requires practice, but must also be practical. We will be working on writing skills which are potentially of use to students right away, such as making lists of needed items or thoughts and filling out a form.

You can help your child at home by letting him or her assist you while you make your grocery list, jot down messages from phone conversations, or even make birthday cards with brief personal messages inside for friends and relatives. Encourage your child to read constantly! The TV guide, sorting your mail, reading words from the shopping mall, signs on the street—everything!

And most important, read to your child every night, if possible.

Sincerely,

_____

Teacher

Skill Sheet #5: Progress Report

+ mastered
√ emerging
− not mastered

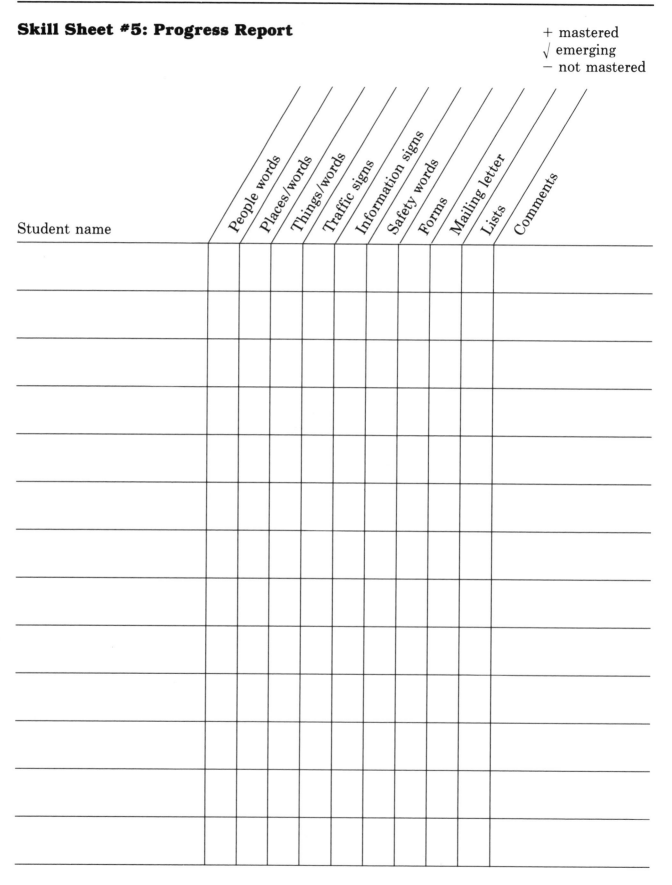

Student name

People words
Places/words
Things/words
Traffic signs
Information signs
Safety words
Forms
Mailing letter
Lists
Comments

I-E BASIC READING AND WRITING SKILLS   *LESSON 36*

WORDS—PEOPLE

Objective:

Given prompts, the student will read/write words depicting people (e.g., family, occupations, important others).

Discussion:

Teacher: I'm going to write some words on the board, and I'd like you to tell me who I am writing about. (Write: Teacher, your full name, your first name if desired) These words all refer to me! Who are some of the most important people in your life? (parents, family, friends) We are going to be working on the skills involved in reading/ writing the words that refer to people. There are many ways to group people. We could group them by family, by friends, by workers, and all kinds of other groups. (See accompanying "Idea List.")

Worksheet I-36 On this worksheet, I want you to think about people who are familiar to you. Everyone's answers may be quite different on this sheet this time. Write down your own people and we'll talk about the many different answers that we find.

Answers: (will vary)

Extension Activities:

1. *People* **Magazine.** Have students create and produce their own personal copy of a magazine with interviews, articles, drawings, and/or collages of important people. They may wish to include a type of glossary at the end, listing the name of the person, some statistics, and a brief explanation of why that person is important to him.

2. **Word Bank (People).** Have students brainstorm and see how extensive a list they can produce for each category of person listed (e.g., famous people, characters, workers). Have them read and/or write the ones that you feel are most important.

Idea List:

PEOPLE WORDS

Family Members

aunt	grandfather	stepfather
brother	grandmother	stepmother
cousin	mother	uncle
father	sister	

Idea List:

PEOPLE WORDS

Friends

Workers

baker
banker
chef
dentist
doctor
engineer
fireman

grocer
librarian
pharmacist
policeman
postman
veterinarian

School Personnel

assistant
bus driver
custodian
principal
teacher

Famous People

authors
government workers
people in the news
sports figures, athletes

Characters

in books
in comic books
in movies
on television
toys or dolls

I–36

WORDS—PEOPLE

Think of the name of a person who would fit the following description. Write his or her name on the line.

1. A person in my family   _____

2. A person who laughs a lot   _____

3. A person who is tall   _____

4. My best friend   _____

5. A person who helps me   _____

6. A person who works in my town   _____

7. A person who is a woman   _____

8. A person who is famous   _____

9. A person who is in the news   _____

10. A person who can do something I wish I could do   _____

11. A person who is not real   _____

12. A cartoon person   _____

13. A person on television   _____

14. A person at school   _____

15. A character in a book or story   _____

I-E BASIC READING AND WRITING SKILLS   *LESSON 37*

WORDS—PLACES

Objective:

Given prompts, the student will read/write words depicting places in the community, their state, and the country.

Discussion:

Teacher: Where would you like to go if I gave you the next hour off? Where would you go if you could go anywhere in our state? Now let's say you have a free airplane ride to any place in the country. Where would I find you? All of those are important places. It's important to be able to read and write the names of those places. Let's group your ideas by community, state, and country. (See accompanying "Idea List.")

Worksheet I-37 Here is a worksheet that will help you practice reading and writing words that tell about places. There may be more than one correct answer for the places described, so think about other choices too.

Answers: (will vary)

Extension Activities:

1. **Community Map.** Have students locate important community places on a map (enlarged, if possible) of your town. They may want to draw or find a picture depicting the place and draw an arrow from the spot on the map to the picture. Arrange for a "walking tour" if your community is close and easily accessible.

2. **Welcome to My State.** Spend some time discussing the noteworthy points of interest in your state. Collect and display brochures, view filmstrips or videos, and if possible take a field trip. Read and review the words associated with these places often.

Idea List:

PLACE WORDS

Community

airport	beauty salon	emergency room
animal shelter	car dealer	fire department
apartments	church	florist shop
appliance store	clothing store	food store
bakery	court house	football field
bank	dentist's office	funeral home
barber shop	doctor's office	furniture store

Idea List:

PLACE WORDS

gas station
golf course
government offices
hardware store
hospital
jewelry store
Laundromat
library
motel
movie theater
newspaper office
nursing home
park
pet store
pizzeria

playground
police station
pool
post office
print shop
restaurant
school
shoe repair
shopping mall
sporting goods store
travel agency
video store
YMCA
zoo

State

(list tourist attractions,
historical sites, the capital
city, other noteworthy places)

United States

the Alamo
Churchill Downs
Disney World and Disneyland
Grand Canyon
Monticello
Niagara Falls
states
Washington, D.C.
White House

Name _____ Date _____

I–37

WORDS—PLACES

Think of the name of a place that would fit each of the following descriptions. Write the place on the line.

1. A place to get help if you get hurt   _____

2. A place to have fun   _____

3. A place to see a movie   _____

4. A place to go to with a friend   _____

5. A place to go to with a parent   _____

6. A place to get a pet   _____

7. A place to show friends who are visiting from far away   _____

8. A place where you can get a postcard   _____

9. A place to get books   _____

10. A place where you'd like to visit for a day   _____

11. A place where you'd like to visit for a week   _____

12. A place where you could get something to eat   _____

13. A place where you could get something for your house   _____

14. A place where you could find the president of the United States   _____

15. A place where you could get something to wear   _____

WORDS—THINGS

Objective:

Given prompts, the student will read/write words depicting things (e..g, animals, clothing, tools, etc.).

Discussion:

Teacher: I am going to give you a category, and I want you to help me list as many words as you can think of that would go in that group. (give categories such as animals, furniture, etc.) These are other words that are important to know how to read and write. (See accompanying "Idea List.") The words that you choose are important, because they are important to you.

Worksheet I-38 Here are some students who want to get some things. Help them list some possible items that might be what they are looking for.

Answers: (will vary)

Extension Activities:

1. **Twenty Questions.** Give students a general category; then have them ask questions (limit to 20) to try to ascertain what the specific object or item is. Write their choices on the board for practice in reading and writing the items. When the answer is reached, reread the guesses and discuss why they were good guesses but not the correct answer.

2. **"Fish."** Make word cards for items in several categories. Deal seven cards randomly to each player. When a player has four words from the same category, he or she can "retire" them and draw new cards from the fishing pile. Winner is the player who has the most sets of word cards when all cards from the fishing pile are gone. (This game may be adapted as needed to fit the number of categories used, players, and words to be learned.)

Idea List:

OBJECTS AND THINGS WORDS

Animals

antelope	iguana	quail
bear	jackal	rooster
cat	kangaroo	squirrel
dog	llama	turtle
elephant	mouse	zebra
goat	octopus	
horse	pony	

Idea List:

OBJECTS AND THINGS WORDS (cont'd)

Tools

chisel
drill
hammer
level
nail
saw
screwdriver

Furniture

bed
chair
couch
desk
dresser
lamp
table

Clothing

bathing suit
belt
coat
dress
jacket
mittens
pants
scarf
shirt
shoes
skirt
socks
underwear
vest

Toys and games

baseball
basketball
coloring book
crayons
dartboard
doll
marbles
model car
modeling clay
paint set

School items

backpack
book
eraser
lunch box
markers
notebook
paper
pen
pencil
ruler

House

attic
basement
bathroom
bathtub
bedroom
carpet
closet
dishwasher
door

kitchen
living room
oven
porch
refrigerator
rug
stove
telephone
television
toilet
typewriter
VCR
window

Food

apple
banana
bread
butter
carrot
cereal
cheese
cookies
crackers
eggs
hamburger
hot dog
lettuce
macaroni
milk
pizza
spaghetti
tomato
turkey

_____

WORDS—THINGS

_____

Help these students make lists of things that would go into the categories.

1. I would like a new pet for my birthday. What are some pets that I might enjoy having?

_____
_____
_____
_____

2. My aunt gave me $15 for my birthday. What are some things I might want to buy?

_____
_____
_____
_____

3. I'm going to a party this weekend. What clothes should I get ready?

_____
_____
_____
_____

4. It's my mom's birthday. What would make a nice gift for her?

_____
_____
_____
_____

5. It's the first day of school. What do I need?

_____
_____
_____
_____

6. I'm so hungry! What might make a great meal?

_____
_____
_____
_____

I-E BASIC READING AND WRITING SKILLS   *LESSON 39*

TRAFFIC SIGNS

Objective:

Given a list of common traffic signs, the student will read and explain each one's use.

Discussion:

Teacher: When you are out walking or riding your bike around town, what are some signs that you see that help you get around? A *traffic* sign is a sign that helps move people or things by showing them which way to go. Why do you think we need signs like that? (might be a lot of traffic, helps everyone know which way to go to avoid accidents)

Worksheet I-39 Here are the words and pictures to ten common traffic signs. Some you would see if you were on your bike or in a car; others you would see if you were walking. Match the sign with the words that tell you what you should do if you see the sign in traffic.

Answers:

1. i	6. a
2. c	7. h
3. d	8. f
4. e	9. g
5. j	10. b

Extension Activities:

1. **Traffic Walk.** If possible, take a community walk and note which traffic signs are common in your area. Have students watch pedestrians and cars and notice whether or not people are following the instructions carefully.

2. **Driving Course.** Have students bring in small toy cars and maneuver them along a student-made "driving course" with traffic signs to direct them. Include a stop sign, a one-way sign, pedestrian crosswalk, and other signs that appear locally.

TRAFFIC SIGNS

Match the traffic sign with the description of what the sign means. Write the letter after the picture of the sign.

1. Bicycle crossing _____

2. Curve left _____

3. Don't walk _____

4. Detour _____

5. Railroad crossing _____

6. Stop _____

7. One way _____

8. S curve _____

9. School crossing _____

10. Yield _____

a. You must come to a complete stop.

b. Go slowly and if there is someone coming to the intersection, let them go first.

c. The road ahead is going to turn to the left.

d. Don't cross the intersection while this is flashing; wait!

e. The usual road is not the way to go; follow the signs for directions to go a different way.

f. The road ahead is going to curve first one way, and then another way.

g. Be careful ahead because children will be crossing the street to get to school.

h. You can only go in one direction on this street.

i. Be careful ahead because people on bicycles will be crossing the street.

j. Be careful ahead because you will be crossing railroad tracks; watch for a train.

INFORMATION SIGNS

Objective:

Given a list of common information signs, the student will read and explain each one's use.

Discussion:

Teacher: Let's say you safely took a bicycle ride through town and wanted to get something to eat. What is a sign that you might see on the door of a restaurant that would help you make a decision about eating at that restaurant? (open/closed; hours) How would you get in the door? (push/pull) What is a sign that you might look for if you needed to wash your hands? (restroom) Today I want you to think about *information* signs—signs that tell you something you need to know.

Worksheet I-40 Here are some situations that you may encounter and some signs that may help you by giving you some information. Read each situation and decide what you will do. Circle *yes* or *no* for each situation.

Answers:

1. Yes	5. No
2. No	6. No
3. No	7. Yes
4. Yes	

Extension Activities:

1. **Information Posters.** Driver's manuals have color pictures of traffic and information signs used along roads. Have students work in teams and draw, enlarge, and color posters to depict helpful signs. Display them around the room and allow students time to explain their use.

2. **Walk Through School.** Have students carefully observe information signs that are displayed throughout the school building. Discuss the purpose of the signs and the information that is conveyed. How many of the signs incorporate pictures to get the message across? (no smoking, handicapped access, etc.)

INFORMATION SIGNS

Here are some information signs and some situations. Circle Yes or No to show how you would use the information to make a decision.

1. ELEVATOR

You want to go to your doctor's office on the tenth floor of a building. Will this sign help you get there?

Yes   No

2. OUT OF ORDER

You are trying to make a phone call to your mother to have her pick you up after school. Will you use this phone?

Yes   No

3. PUSH

You want to go inside the video store, but the door won't open. Are you pushing on the door?

Yes   No

4. SELF-SERVE

You are in line to get a drink and a sandwich at a cafeteria. You are waiting for the man behind the counter to help you, but he isn't even looking at you. Are you supposed to reach in and get your own food?

Yes   No

5. NO TRESPASSING

Your toy airplane flew over the fence and landed in a yard with this sign in front. Will you climb the fence to get your plane?

Yes   No

6. EXACT CHANGE NEEDED

You want to buy a candy bar from a vending machine. All you have is a dollar bill. Can you get a candy bar here?

Yes   No

7. CLOSED

You want to play pinball at the arcade, but the door won't open. Should you come back at a different time?

Yes   No

I-E BASIC READING AND WRITING SKILLS   *LESSON 41*

SAFETY WORDS

Objective:

Given a list of common safety words, the student will read and explain each one's use.

Discussion:

Teacher: There is one more group of words that we are going to make sure you understand and can read. These are *safety* words. (See accompanying "Idea List.") Safety words help you stay out of danger. Can anyone think of any helpful safety words? (beware of dog, poison) When would you see these words?

   Worksheet I-41 See if you can figure out what the message is from these safety words. On the lines, write what you think might happen if someone didn't read or understand the safety words.

Answers: (will vary)

(examples)

   1. Might touch something that would shock them
   2. Might get hit by a car
   3. Might get trapped in a building on fire
   4. Might not be able to put out a fire in time
   5. Might eat or drink something that could make you very sick
   6. Might get bitten by a dog
   7. Might get paint all over your hands or clothes
   8. Might not notify fire department in time
   9. Something might catch on fire if you aren't careful with matches
   10. Might get lost or stuck in the wrong place
   11. Might burn yourself
   12. Might trip down the steps

Extension Activities:

   1. **The Safety Match Game.** Make two copies of each of the safety words on durable cards. Flip the cards over and scatter them on a flat surface. Have students take turns turning over two at a time. If the cards match, the student takes them and takes another turn. Winner is the student with the most pairs of cards.

2. **Safety Coloring Book.** Assign each student a safety word to write carefully and to illustrate with a simple picture or cartoon depicting someone not following the safety instruction. Reproduce and collate everyone's contribution and assemble into a class coloring book of safety words.

Idea List:

SIGN AND SAFETY WORDS

Traffic signs

bicycle crossing
curve left/right
detour
do not enter
do not pass
don't walk/walk
keep left/right
one way
pedestrian crossing
railroad crossing
rest stop
S curve
school crossing
stop
yield

Information signs

elevator
entrance
exact change needed
men/women
no trespassing
open/closed
out of order
phone
please pay cashier
please wait to be seated

push/pull
quiet
rest rooms
self-serve
up/down
use other door

Safety words

beware of dog
caution
caution—wet floor
danger-keep out
do not enter
don't walk
emergency exit
exit
fire alarm
fire extinguisher
flammable
hot/cold
keep off
no smoking
on/off
poison
police
stairs
watch your step

I–41

SAFETY WORDS

Here are some safety words. What could happen if you didn't read or understand the words? Write your answers on the lines.

1. DANGER—KEEP OUT

_____

2. DON'T WALK

_____

3. EXIT

_____

4. FIRE EXTINGUISHER

_____

5. POISON

_____

6. BEWARE OF DOG

_____

7. WET PAINT

_____

8. FIRE ALARM

_____

9. FLAMMABLE

_____

10. DO NOT ENTER

_____

11. HOT

_____

12. WATCH YOUR STEP

_____

FILLING OUT A FORM

Objective:

Given a sample form requesting basic information, the student will clearly and accurately complete the form.

Discussion:

Teacher: Earlier, we talked about being able to tell someone what your name is, your address, and other important information. Why is it important to be able to do that? (to get help, keep careful records) Why do you think it might be important to read and write that information too? (don't have to keep repeating it, send it to someone through the mail) What are some examples where you might have to fill out a form that needs that information? (going to camp, sending away for something, school records)

Worksheet I-42 Have you ever won a million dollars? Someday maybe that will happen to you, so to prepare you for that, you are going to fill out a practice form. If you are unsure of some of the information (area code, school address), think about how you could find the answers. (ask, use phone book, school secretary) Remember to write clearly. Why? (so people at other end can send the prize to the correct address)

Answers: (will vary)

Extension Activities:

1. **Forms and More Forms.** Have students begin collecting forms that require writing their address and other basic information. They may include send-away forms from cereal boxes, comic books, and other sources.

2. **Raffle.** Have students complete a class-made form for a chance at winning a (small) raffle prize. Students may include information that they think is important to know, such as favorite movie character, shoe size, number of pets, and so on. Make it fun!

FILLING OUT A FORM

You have just been given a chance to win $1,000,000! The specially marked box of cereal that you had your breakfast from this morning has a winning ticket. Fill out the following form clearly and correctly!

YES!

My name is _____

My address is _____
             (number)   (street)

_____
      (city)   (state)   (zip)

My phone number is _____
            (area code)

My date of birth is _____

My parents' names are _____
          (father)

_____
         (mother)

I go to school at _____
         (name)

_____
      (city)   (state)   (zip)

This is what I would like to do if I win the $1,000,000 prize: _____

_____

_____

I-E BASIC READING AND WRITING SKILLS   *LESSON 43*

MAILING A LETTER

Objective:

The student will correctly address an envelope, apply a stamp, and mail a letter to a recipient.

Discussion:

Teacher: Has anyone received their prize of $1,000,000 yet? Why not? (didn't send out forms) What do you think we should do next to make sure you get your price? (send the form) If we wanted to mail a letter, is it enough to just stick it in a mailbox? What else do we need to do? (stamp, et cetera) The steps for mailing that letter include (1) address the envelope, (2) put your return address, (3) put on a stamp, and (4) mail the letter.

Worksheet I-43 These students are all sending away for something or writing a letter that they wish to mail. Each, however, has run into a problem. Look over the steps for mailing a letter and write down the number of the step that is a problem. Then we'll discuss how to correct it so the students can get their letter in the mail.

Answers:

1. 2 (return address)
2. 3 (stamp)
3. 4 (mailed it in a trash can)
4. 1 (address)
5. 3 (stamp)
6. 2 (return address)

Extension Activities:

1. **Mail Call.** Have students complete one of the forms from the previous lesson and actually send it through the mail to obtain something or some information. (You may wish to find some inexpensive items or free information that would be interesting for them to receive.) Walk to the post office or nearest mailbox and deposit each letter.

2. **Letters to Dracula.** Have students select one of several cartoon characters, sports heroes, or someone appealing to the student. After writing a letter, have students complete an envelope (possibly including a sticker for a stamp if you don't intend to actually mail them), and "mail" them. You may wish to have students answer each other's letters (in character, of course).

MAILING A LETTER

Each of the students below wants to mail a letter, but each has a problem with one of the four steps. Write the number of the problem that needs to be corrected.

    1 = address the envelope
    2 = return address
    3 = stamp
    4 = mail the letter

1. Ron sent away for a set of comic books. He filled out the form, put it in the envelope, wrote the address, put on a stamp, and took it to the post office. He didn't get his comic books. What was the problem?

             _____

2. Sandy wrote a letter to her best friend. She carefully put her address in the top corner, wrote her friend's address on the front, and put it in her mailbox with the flag up. What's wrong?

             _____

3. Jennifer sent away for a set of coloring markers. She put a label on that had her address printed on it, wrote out the address, put on a stamp, and put the letter in a large metal box. What's the problem?

             _____

4. Randy put a stamp on his letter, wrote his return address, and put the letter in the mailbox on the corner. What was the problem with this letter?

             _____

5. This is the letter that Debbie sent to a toy company. What was the problem?

             _____

6. Maria was in a hurry to get her order for a new game in the mail. What's wrong with this letter?

             _____

MAKING LISTS

Objective:

Given a category or situation, the student will compose an appropriate list of needed items or people.

Discussion:

Teacher: I'm having a party at my house, and I want you to go to the store and get me these things: 2 quarts of milk, 8 pounds of hamburger, 6 bananas, 1 quart of strawberries, 2 cans of whipped cream, 8 hot dogs, 1 loaf of bread, 3 bags of potato chips—wait! How are you going to remember all that? (list) Unless you've got a memory like a tape recorder, you might need to make lists of things that you need to remember.

Worksheet I-44 Now you are going to pretend that you are in some situations where you will find a list helpful. Write your answers in the space after each situation.

Answers: (will vary)

Extension Activities:

1. **How Many Can You List?** Call out a topic (or choose one randomly from a pile) and have students list as many items that would go with that topic in 60 (or 30) seconds. Topics may include animals, girls' names, words that start with "b," kinds of dogs, kids in the class, baseball teams, and so on.

2. **Rotating List.** A variation on the first activity is having one student begin the list, passing the list to the next student, and continuing on until each student has had at least one turn. How many items can you include for a given topic? If a child is stuck, you could have students with other ideas give clues, so that everyone is still thinking (even when it isn't their turn). The student with the list should call out his or her answer before writing it down to make sure the group agrees that it belongs on the list. Good discussions may follow!

MAKING LISTS

Here are some situations for which you may have to make a list. Write down the items that would be on your list.

1. You are having a birthday party at your house. Your mother wants to know who you would like to invite. Who's on your list?

2. You just got a check for $100 in the mail with instructions that you have to spend it TODAY or lose it all! Quick! Make a list of at least five things that you're going to buy.

3. You turned into Santa Claus for a day and have to make a list (and check it twice) of what you're going to get for all of the members of your family. What's on the list?

HO!
HO!
HO!

4. Your teacher wants you to list as many zoo animals as you can think of in 60 seconds. GO!

5. You're going shopping for food for that birthday party you're having. What are you going to get?

6. Your rock group, The Ninja Cows, is going on tour. You want to line up some important places to play. Make your list of where you'll be playing.

PARENT LETTER #6   STRESS MANAGEMENT

Dear Parents,

Ever feel overwhelmed because you have too much to do, too little time, you're not sure how to do it anyway, and you feel ready to POP? Sometimes your child can feel that way too, and being a child, he or she may not be able to think through the problem and come up with a better solution than crying, hitting, or developing an ulcer. (Of course, sometimes as adults we end up that way too!)

We are going to be talking about stress—what it is, how to deal with it,—and trying out ways to reduce those feelings. You know your child better than anyone. Perhaps you have some techniques for handling these problems that work well at home with your child. Please feel free to share your insights with us. When talking to your child at home, especially during times of conflict, stress, and "falling apart," emphasize that there are ways to cope with pressure and proceed to show and tell your child how. It may be as simple as changing activities, hitting a pillow, or taking a few deep breaths or as complex as needing to talk to someone right away. Let your child know that you are his or her best resource; that you care about him or her, will listen to him or her, and will try to understand him or her. Life is hard enough. We all need someone.

Let's help each other.

Sincerely,

_____

Teacher

I-F   STRESS MANAGEMENT

Skill Sheet #6: Progress Report

+ mastered
√ emerging
− not mastered

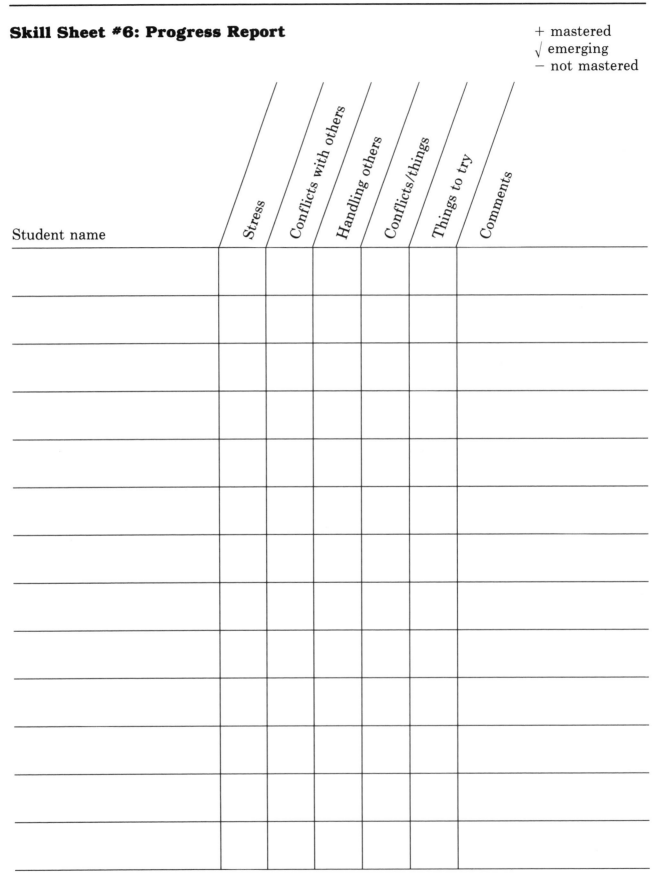

Student name	Stress	Conflicts with others	Handling others	Conflicts/things	Things to try	Comments

WHAT IS STRESS?

Objective:

The student will define and explain examples of stress.

Discussion:

Teacher: We're going to be talking about something called *stress* in the next few lessons, in particular the feeling called stress. Does anyone know what "stress" means? It's the feeling that you might get when someone yells at you, or you have 20 things to do and only 2 minutes to do them all, or you're very angry about something—so angry that your stomach turns into little knots and you might find it hard to breathe and your body just doesn't know what to do. In other words, stress is a feeling of tenseness and pressure caused by something you are worried about.

Worksheet I-45 On this worksheet, you will find some students who are feeling stress or worry from situations. Circle the students who are feeling stress. Then we'll talk about why they might feel that way.

Answers:

1. Circle
2. Don't circle
3. Circle
4. Circle
5. Don't circle
6. Circle

Extension Activities:

1. **Picture of Stress.** Have students look through magazines to find pictures of facial expressions that indicate stress. Students may want to practice looking in a mirror while making faces and try to draw what a stressful face looks like.

2. **Stress Synonyms.** Make a large poster with the word STRESS written or drawn in large letters. Have students contribute synonyms for stress and write the words on the poster (e.g., fear, worry, pain, sweaty, scared, knots in stomach).

I–45

WHAT IS STRESS?

Some of these students are feeling stress. Circle the ones who are feeling tense and worried about something.

1. Oh, no... it's almost my turn to stand up in front of the whole class and read my report. What if everyone laughs at me? What if I mess up?

2. Oh good! It's almost my turn to bat. I'm going to hit a home run!

3. The door is locked! How will I get in? What did I do with that stupid key? Oh, no!

4. The bus is here! Hurry up! It's not going to wait for you! Get moving! Where are your shoes???

5. I have a lot of homework to do... but I'll grab a snack first and then sit right down and do it. I can get it all done.

6. I'll meet you after school, punk, behind the woods. Then you'll pay for eating my candy bar.

But it was an accident...

I-F STRESS MANAGEMENT   *LESSON 46*

CONFLICTS WITH OTHERS

Objective:

The student will identify situations which may cause conflict between people and lead to stress.

Discussion:

Teacher: Who can give me some examples of situations that cause stress? (review yesterday's lesson) A major source of stress is "people stress," or conflicts with others. When you have a fight or misunderstanding with another person, those feelings don't just go away. Sometimes they hang around and make you feel stress or stressed out. Today we're going to take a look at stress between or caused by other people.

Worksheet I-46 The people on this sheet are usually right in the middle of conflicts or arguments with others. Read about them and match the person with the explanation of how they may cause others to feel stress.

Answers:

    1. b
    2. c
    3. d
    4. e
    5. a

Extension Activities:

1. **Stressful Situations with Others.** Without getting *too* personal, have students tell about times when they felt stressed because of an experience with another person. Discuss reasons why a person may "take it out" on another person.

2. **Role Playing.** Have students who volunteer play the "bad guy" in role playing the students on the worksheet. Discuss with the class how such a person would make them feel. (The following lesson discusses reactions to the feelings, so you may not want to go beyond the feelings with this role play.)

CONFLICTS WITH OTHERS

These people are looking for trouble by causing stressful situations for others (and themselves). Match the person with the letter that tells why he or she has trouble getting along with others.

a. Wants to fight without listening to an explanation.

1. _Share?? You want me to share my stuff? Forget it—you can't even touch my stuff!_ _____

b. Greedy, doesn't want to share anything.

2. _I'm bigger and stronger than you so stay out of my way!_ _____

3. _So you got an A on your test? You must think you're pretty smart. So what?_ _____
People who are smart are boring and brag all the time.

c. Threatens people; thinks that if you are big and tough, that makes you right.

4. _When did you get glasses? Boy, you look really stupid._ _____

d. Puts other people down for something they can do; is probably jealous.

5. _You took my pencil without asking. I'm going to punch your lights out. Look out!_ _____

e. Makes fun of others; says unkind things (especially when the other person can't help the situation).

HANDLING CONFLICTS WITH OTHERS

Objective:

The student will be able to list or state at least three appropriate ways to handle conflicts with others.

Discussion:

Teacher: Today we're going to talk a bit more about conflicts with others that cause stress. How do those kinds of conflicts make you feel? (discuss feelings of stress) Can you always control what other people do to end the conflict? (no) Can you sometimes control what *you* do to handle the conflict? What you do may not put an end to the problem, but how you handle yourself—what you do in the situation—may turn things around. At the very least, if you handle yourself appropriately, you can feel better about yourself, knowing that you did the best you could do. What are some ways that you have handled a stressful situation with others?

Worksheet I-47 There are many different ways to handle a stressful situation with others. Sometimes something will work one time with a person, and sometimes you have to keep trying until you find something that works. On this worksheet, write *yes* or *no* if you think the student is doing the right thing.

Answers:

1. Yes
2. No
3. No
4. Yes
5. Yes
6. Yes
7. No
8. Yes

Extension Activities:

1. **Let's Try . . . .** Have students as a group make a list of many different ways to resolve the conflicts with others that cause them stress. Students could make posters illustrating their ideas.
2. **Role Playing.** Have students role play the situations portrayed on Worksheets I-46 and I-47 to "try out" the responses suggested. Which do they feel comfortable with?

HANDLING CONFLICTS WITH OTHERS

Some of these students are handling conflicts with others in a way that will help to end the conflict or at least help the problem become smaller. Write *yes* or *no* if you think the student is doing the right thing or not.

1. Well, if you don't want to share, that's fine. I'll do something else. _____

2. You want to fight me? Fine. I'll go get a hammer and you'll see a real fight! _____

3. Don't laugh at me for having glasses. Your braces and pimples make you look like something from outer space. _____

4. I don't want to get in trouble for fighting. Please leave me alone and we'll drop it. If you don't, I will talk to my teacher and my parents. _____

5. I won't say anything to her. I'll just turn and walk away. _____

6. I don't like it that you make fun of me for being smart. I will continue to do my best in school. What you say is not going to stop me from doing what I know is right. _____

7. QUIT YELLING AT ME! STOP IT! I DON'T LIKE YOU YELLING ALL THE TIME! _____

8. Instead of being so nasty to us, why don't you join us in a game of soccer? Let's play and have some fun. _____

CONFLICTS WITH THINGS

Objective:

Given a stressful situation, the student will identify the source of the conflict or probable fear.

Discussion:

Teacher: We've talked about dealing with stress caused by other people. What about the girl who was nervous about making a speech in front of her class? What was causing the stress there? (fear of others laughing) What about the boy who was feeling stress because the bus was there and he didn't have his books and clothes organized? (fear of being late, being left) And what about the girl who couldn't get her door open? What caused her stress? (fear of not being able to get in) Stress can also be brought on by situations—not enough time, not enough money, not being organized, and so on. Today we're going to think about those kinds of stresses.

Worksheet I-48 These students are feeling stress because they are afraid of something—something that may or may not happen. Help each student figure out what their fear or fears might be. Write your answer in the second column. Then we'll discuss them.

Answers:

(examples)

1. Fear of a bad grade, reprimands by teacher
2. Fear of not being able to get the book, having lost money
3. Fear of others laughing, hurting grandmother's feelings
4. Fear that people don't like her (this is more of a fear about other people than a conflict between other people, as in Lesson 46)
5. Fear of having lost all that time, wasted effort, bad grade
6. Fear that dog might die
7. Fear of parents' reprimands, fear of not getting everything done in time

Extension Activities:

1. **Sad Stories.** Have students pick one of the situations on the worksheet and develop it into a short story. Have them set up the situation, describe the feelings of the main character, and emphasize the fear that is a part of the stress. Students can save the stories for a day or two and then have multiple endings written by other students following Lesson 49, which explores handling stressful situations.

2. **Paperback Time.** There are many excellent paperback stories written for elementary students emphasizing problems, conflicts, and situations typically faced by this age group. Have students select one and make time to read it out loud to the class every day, perhaps right before or after lunch. Students of all ages love to be read to, and this can tie in nicely with discussions of stress and conflict resolution.

I-48

CONFLICTS WITH THINGS

The students below are feeling stressed because of situations they are in. Help each student figure out what the fear of their conflict is by filling in the second column with your ideas.

Situation Fear(s)

1. Oh no! I can't believe I forgot to do my homework!

2. I'm supposed to have $2 for the books I ordered, but I only have $1.

3. Why do I have to wear that silly-looking dress that my grandmother bought me? I hate it!

4. Why won't Erin and Jenny talk to me? Is it because I made the volleyball team and they didn't? I can't help it that sports are so easy for me!

5. I spent five hours painting my art project, and now the rain has ruined everything!

6. My poor dog is at the vet while I'm here in math class. What if she doesn't make it through the surgery?

7. I have to mow the grass, wash the car, and clean my room—all before my parents get home in one hour! Why didn't I start sooner????

THINGS TO TRY

Objective:

The student will identify at least three techniques or strategies that he could employ in a stressful situation.

Discussion:

Teacher: Nobody can get away from stress; there are things in everyone's life that are hard for them to cope with. But people usually find ways to deal with stress in healthy ways. Today's worksheet shows you some ways that might help you reduce your stress.

Worksheet I-49 Here are some ideas to help you when you find yourself in a stressful situation. We will discuss them all; then I want you to circle ones that you think you could try.

Extension Activities:

1. **Class Jogging.** Prepare the class a day ahead of time for a jog around the playground or engage in another noncompetitive activity for purposes of relaxation and relieving stress. Class biking or a similar activity could also be introduced.

2. **Meet Your Counselor.** Make sure your students know where the counselor's office is and what services he or she can provide. If possible, have him or her talk to your class about why a counselor is in the school. Many schools have at least part-time elementary counselors who have groups that meet on a regular basis.

3. **Be a Balloon.** There are numerous stress-reducing activities which can help a student become familiar with the feelings of stress in his or her body and techniques to reduce them. For example, have the students relax by lying on the floor with eyes shut. Then have them tense sets of muscles or areas of the body for several seconds; then allow the muscles to relax. Tell them to think of becoming a balloon, being blown up, and then slowly compressed and emptied. Kids will think it's fun.

THINGS TO TRY

Here are some ideas for handling stress when you feel those stressful feelings—whether they are from people or situations. Circle the ones that you would like to try.

Go for a walk . . . leave the stressful situation.

Do something active. Play basketball or go running!

Tense and relax: Make your whole body tense up . . . then relax it little by little (like letting the air slowly out of a balloon).

Talk to a friend. Tell a friend what's on your mind.

Talk to an adult who can help you—a parent, a teacher, a counselor, the parent of a friend, a pastor.

Prepare! Plan ahead. Lots of stressful situations can be overcome by being ready for anything that can go wrong.

Breathe and think. Take a few moments to calm down; then make a plan for another way to handle the problem.

part II

Personal Independence

PARENT LETTER #7 CLOTHING AND DRESSING

Dear Parents,

Part of personal independence is knowing how to dress, when to dress a certain way, and how to care for clothing. We will be working on skills related to clothing appropriate for particular situations.

There are several ways you can help your child as we progress through this unit. First, if your child can dress himself or herself, allow him or her to do so (even if the clothes don't always match!). You may want to provide the final "once over" to make sure your child is presentable. Give your child choices as to what he or she will wear, reminding him or her to think about the weather, the temperature, the conditions of the place that he or she will be going to (inside? heated? muddy?), and how careful he or she needs to be to keep his or her clothes clean.

Cleanliness! Another thought! When you are doing the laundry, let your child watch and help, even if it's just a matter of pairing up socks or tossing in the detergent. Children need to see the complete process of wearing–cleaning– putting away– and wearing again.

When you shop for clothes, ask your child's opinion about the clothes you get for him or her. Make him or her think about warmth, and style, of course, as well as cost. Expose your child to your thoughts about buying something to wear—what goes through your mind?

Happy shopping!

Sincerely,

_____

Teacher

Skill Sheet #7: Progress Report

+ mastered
√ emerging
− not mastered

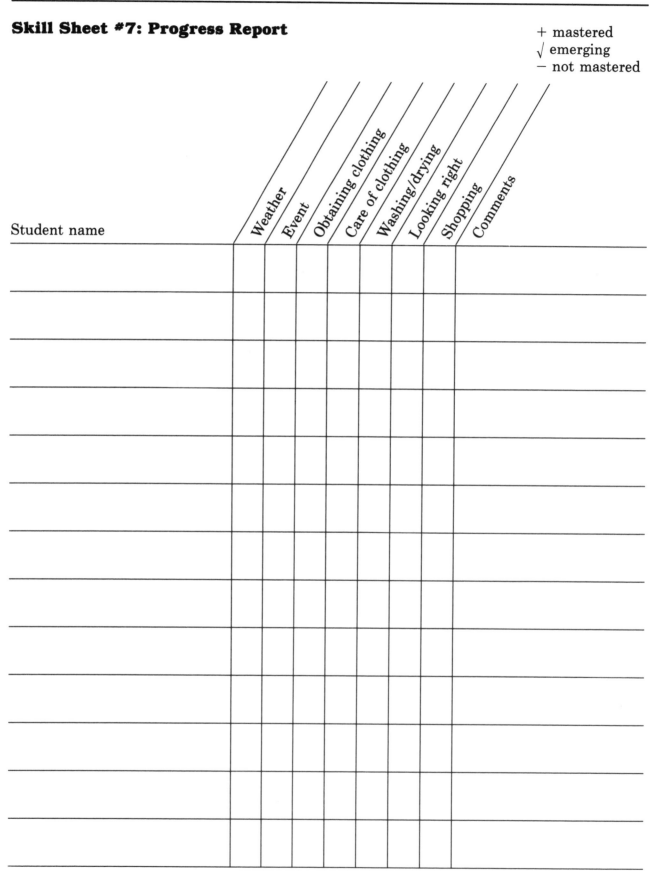

Student name	Weather	Event	Obtaining clothing	Care of clothing	Washing/drying	Looking right	Shopping	Comments

© 1992 by The Center for Applied Research in Education

WHAT'S THE WEATHER?

Objective:

The student will identify appropriate clothing suitable for weather conditions.

Discussion:

Teacher: It's snowing outside, so I better get my swimming suit and my umbrella. What are you laughing at? Is there something wrong with my choice of clothing? We are going to be talking about clothes for a few days. One thing that you should keep in mind about clothes is the weather. What kinds of clothing would you wear in very cold weather? (warm, sweaters, extra layers) What would you wear in hot weather? (shorts, T-shirts, swimsuits, etc.)

Worksheet II-50 What you wear each day depends a lot on the weather. Read the weather reports in the worksheet and circle each item that you could wear on that day.

Answers:

1. Shorts, tennis shoes
2. Raincoat, light jacket
3. Shorts, T-shirt
4. Jacket, hat, boots
5. Shoes, mittens, jacket
6. Heavy jacket, socks
7. Sweater, long-sleeved shirt, pants

Extension Activities:

1. **Weather Girl.** Have students listen to the weather report on the evening news. Does the weather forecaster give advice on what to wear? You may bring in a large doll (or mannequin) and have students "dress" the prop according to the weather.

2. **Season Sort.** Collect numerous pictures from magazines of people dressed in seasonal clothing. Mount them on construction paper, shuffle them, and have students sort them according to their dress for the seasons.

WHAT'S THE WEATHER?

Here is the weather report for certain days in your city. Circle each item that would be appropriate to wear on that day.

1. Today will be very hot with a high near 92 degrees. It will be sunny and sticky.

   mittens   boots   shorts   tennis shoes

2. It is going to rain most of the day.

   ear muffs   raincoat   light jacket   thermal underwear

3. It will be pleasant and sunny today, about 75 degrees. No rain in sight!

   shorts   winter coat   T-shirt   scarf

4. Today will be cold, windy, and snowy. Expect 2 to 4 inches of the white stuff!

   shorts   jacket   hat   boots

5. No snow today, but it will be very windy and cold.

   shoes   mittens   sunglasses   jacket

6. It will be about 20 degrees today and cloudy.

   light jacket   heavy jacket   socks   shorts

7. Today will be sunny, windy, and cold, with a high temperature of 40 degrees.

   sweater   long-sleeved shirt   flip-flops   pants

WHAT'S THE EVENT?

Objective:

The student will identify appropriate clothing suitable for social events.

Discussion:

Teacher: Do you remember the story of Cinderella? What was her problem with going to the ball? (didn't have any fancy clothes) Why was it important to her to have a nice dress? (look right) Would Cinderella wear that dress to a baseball game? It's a ball gown, right? (no, not that kind of ball) Why do people have different kinds of clothes for certain events? (feel more comfortable, look better, etc.)

Worksheet II-51 On this worksheet, you are going to match each student who is going to an event with the proper clothing that he or she should wear. Think about why certain clothes are all right for some places, but not for others, such as school.

Answers:

1.	d	5.	a
2.	f	6.	g
3.	h	7.	b
4.	c	8.	e

Extension Activities:

1. **Fouled-up Fairy Tale.** Have students rewrite familiar fairy tales, only have them mix up the clothing that the characters wear. For example, how would Cinderella have ended if the fairy godmother had dressed her in Halloween clothes? What if the seven dwarfs wore baseball uniforms? Or if Little Red Riding Hood's red coat was at the dry cleaner's one day and she wore a policewoman's uniform?

2. **Spirit Week.** Schools often have a "spirit week" in which each day of the week calls for some sort of specific dress; for example, clash day (wear items that do not go together), twin day (wear identical clothes with a friend), colors day (wear all of one color), and so forth. Designate one week as such and include sports day, dress-up day, favorite character from a book day, and so on.

WHAT'S THE EVENT?

These students are going to attend certain events. Match each student with the clothing that would fit each occasion. Write the letter on the blank next to each situation.

1. Alberto is going to play football with the team after school.   _____

2. Cynthia is going to her cousin's wedding.   _____

3. Benjamin has been invited to a swimming party.   _____

4. April is going to a slumber party.   _____

5. Danny is going horseback riding.   _____

6. Vincent is going to a Halloween dance at school.   _____

7. Ricky is hiking around the lake.   _____

8. Maria is going biking in the country.   _____

a.

b.

c.

d.

e.

f.

g.

h.

OBTAINING CLOTHING

Objective:

The student will specify several appropriate places where clothing may be obtained.

Discussion:

Teacher: Why do people have to get new clothes from time to time? (outgrow them, rip them, seasons change, fads change) Why don't you wear clothes like your mother or father wear? Do any of you ever hear complaints from older people about the clothes you wear? Sometimes you really do need to get new or different clothes. Where do they come from? Does everyone get clothes from a store? Do people ever get clothes from each other? (handing down within a family, thrift shop, trading with a friend)

Worksheet II-52 The students on this sheet are all wearing something that is new or different for them. Each got some item of clothing at a different place or source. Write on the line the place where each got clothing.

Answers:

1. Sisters
2. Gift from relatives
3. Retail store
4. Sporting event
5. Sew one herself

Extension Activities:

1. **Did People Really Dress Like That?** Bring in pictures from the "olden days" such as the turn of the century, showing the ornate hats the women wore, elaborate clothing (especially the women's), and ties. Check out a book from the library on how styles have changed over the years. Ask students how they would feel about wearing something like that today!

2. **Fashion Fads.** Each generation has had its own clothing fads. Have students ask their parents about bell bottoms, nehru jackets, go-go boots, and other fashion fads from an earlier time. Old yearbook pictures are another source of some good laughs and discussion.

OBTAINING CLOTHING

These students got some of their clothes from different sources. Read each situation and write on the line the place where each got clothing.

1. I am the youngest of three girls. When I outgrow my sweater, I sometimes can get different sweaters without even going out of my house. Where did I get my sweaters?

   _____

2. It's my birthday! My aunt and uncle really came through with a great present! Guess where my new jeans and jacket came from?

   _____

3. I've got $20 in my purse. My friend and I are heading to the mall to look at some skirts. Where do you think I will get one?

   _____

4. Dad and I went to a football game at the county stadium to watch a professional team. I wanted a sweatshirt with the name of my team on it. Where did I get this?

   _____

5. I have a sewing machine. Next time I want a new vest, what do you think I'll do to get one?

   _____

CARE OF CLOTHING

Objective:

The student will identify several appropriate ways to care for clothing items to ensure longer wear.

Discussion:

Teacher: Why does your mother tell you to take off your good clothes after church and put play clothes on? (so won't get them dirty, torn, etc.) Do your parents ever yell at you for not picking your clothes off the floor? Why? These are ways that you can take care of your clothes so they will last longer and give you more years of wear. Can you think of other ways?

Worksheet II-53 Some of the students on this worksheet are showing ways to take care of their clothes. Others are being careless. Circle the student in each pair who is being careful.

Answers:

1. Second student
2. First student
3. First student
4. Second student

Extension Activities:

1. **How Much Does It Cost?** Have students calculate the average price of a pair of jeans or casual outfit. Then estimate how long the average outfit is worn. What does the daily, weekly, or monthly cost come out to? Is it greater than or less than students thought?

2. **Real Practice.** Give students a demonstration and practice time in clothing care habits such as washing in a washing machine, sewing on buttons, folding and hanging up clothes. They may be surprised to find that it is not as hard as it seems. And practice makes perfect.

CARE OF CLOTHING

These students were told to take good care of their clothes. Circle the student in each pair who is doing something to help take care of his or her clothes.

WASHING AND DRYING CLOTHES

Objective:

The student will identify the appropriate cleaning procedure for different types of clothing articles.

Discussion:

Teacher: If you fell on a day when the snow was melting and your winter coat got all muddy, how would you clean it? Would you throw it in the washing machine? (probably too big, bulky) Would you hang it out on the line to dry? (too cold to dry it) Different kinds of clothing articles require different kinds of cleaning methods. But all kinds of clothes need to be cleaned when they are dirty or have been worn for a while. Let's think about different ways to wash and dry clothes to get them clean.

Worksheet II-54 This page shows some items that would need to be cleaned and different ways that you could clean them. Read the clues carefully to find the answer that matches and write the letter on the line.

Answers:

1.	d	5.	f
2.	g	6.	a
3.	e	7.	h
4.	c	8.	b

Extension Activities:

1. **Visit to Dry Cleaners.** If possible, arrange a visit to a local dry cleaner establishment and have the personnel explain the dry cleaning process to the students. Ask how different types of stains are removed and how cleaning is achieved without water.

2. **Laundry Experiments.** Have students identify laundry products that claim to get rid of common stains. Set up and carry out simple experiments in class comparing different products and their performance in getting out the same stain. Use old towels or T-shirts to receive stains such as mud, blood, magic markers, and so on. Be sure to have students keep accurate records and carry out comparison procedures carefully.

WASHING AND DRYING CLOTHES

Match each item below with a good way to get it clean. Read the clues carefully to find the best matches. Write the letter of your choice on the line.

_____ 1. Heavy wool sweater

_____ 2. T-shirt

_____ 3. Jeans

_____ 4. Towels

_____ 5. Delicate socks or pantyhose

_____ 6. Very nice suit

_____ 7. Sweat socks

_____ 8. Tennis shoes

a. Take it to a dry cleaner; they will clean it without damaging it and probably put it on a hanger.

b. They can be cleaned by hand with a rag and some polish.

c. They can be put in a washing machine and then a dryer; then folded and put into a closet or bathroom.

d. This should be taken to a dry cleaner so that it can be cleaned without shrinking, since this material tends to shrink.

e. This material can shrink too, but after the first washing, it usually will be the same size; you can wash these in a washing machine and then put them in a dryer or hang them out to dry.

f. Wash these out by hand in a sink or tub so the washing machine won't rip them up.

g. Since you probably wear this over and over, just throw it in a washing machine and then a dryer for cleaning; it's easy to care for.

h. These are tough too, and can be cleaned the same way as (g).

LOOKING RIGHT

Objective:

The student will identify characteristics of a person who is neat in appearance.

Discussion:

Teacher: Have you ever heard anyone say, "He looks like such a slob?" What were they referring to? What makes a person look like a slob? What's the opposite of being a slob? (students may say being a "nerd") If you really wanted to look messy, how would you do it? Are there ever times when it's important to look your best?

Worksheet II-55 Whether you like it or not, sometimes it is important and a sign of respect to dress in a manner that shows you can dress carefully and properly for the occasion. This student is about to meet someone important—but he sure doesn't look like it! How could you help him improve his appearance? Circle every part that you think could be improved.

Answers:

Messy hair, comb left in hair, glasses tilted, chewing gum, tie untied, buttons unbuttoned, shirt buttoned wrong, sleeves uneven, torn and dirty pants, shoe untied, one shoe off, dirty sock

Extension Activities:

1. **Milton the Messy.** Have students draw their own version of a messy, unkempt student. By exaggerating the negative, you will have good discussions about what is inappropriate.

2. **Neat for a Day.** Have students designate one day as "Neatnik Day." Have them prepare a checklist—starting from clean hair going to tied shoes—and spend time really grooming themselves. Reward students' efforts by having a party and games, perhaps an award for the "most dignified student." Students will also enjoy exaggerated politeness—lots of "thank you's," "charmed to assist you's," and so on.

LOOKING RIGHT

This student is not looking his best right now. How many things can you find that could help him look better? Circle every part that could be improved.

LET'S GO SHOPPING!

Objective:

The student will state which characteristics are important when shopping for clothing items.

Discussion:

Teacher: When you go shopping for something, why can't you get anything you want? (may not have enough money, not your size) If your mom or dad sent you to shop for shoes for school, what might you come home with? (name-brand tennis shoes, loafers) What would they say if you came home with ski boots? (go right back) So when you go shopping for clothing, what are some things you should keep in mind? (cost, size, value, etc.)

Worksheet II-56 Here are examples of students who were not good shoppers. Can you figure out why? Read each situation and write your answer on the line.

Answers:

1. Spent too much
2. Poor quality
3. Only bought one item
4. Wrong size
5. Not appropriate for all those places
6. Not appropriate for school
7. Too expensive
8. Wrong season

Extension Activities:

1. **Catalog Shopping.** Give each student $100 in "fake" bills. Assign each the task of back-to-school shopping. What items did they buy through the catalog? How did each spend their money? What can you get for $100?

2. **Tennis Shoe Survey.** Have students conduct an informal survey of members of the class, members in a certain grade level, all girls, and so on to determine which brand of tennis shoe is the most popular. You may also include a question concerning where most students purchase their shoes. Keep all respondents anonymous!

SHOPPING FOR CLOTHES

These students were sent shopping for clothes. Why weren't they good shoppers? Write your answer on the line next to each situation.

1. Beth's sister gave her $20 to buy a new skirt.

2. Ronald wanted some jeans that would last a long time.

3. Kate had $100 to get several outfits for school. This is what she came home with.

4. Fred really liked the color of this sweater.

5. Frank wanted to get some shoes that he could wear to school, at home, and on the football team.

6. Sally looked at three different dresses for school. She got the one in the middle.

7. Kris does not have a lot of extra money. She bought the shoes in the middle.

8. Ramon went shopping for some clothes that he could wear outside in the snow.

© 1992 by The Center for Applied Research in Education

Dear Parents,

We will be working on the different skills involved in keeping yourself clean, including taking a bath or shower, caring for hair, cleaning hands and face, and brushing teeth. Your help is needed to reinforce these skills at home. Whatever method of maintaining cleanliness is used, it must be consistently followed every day. To a great extent, the way you want your child to look is influenced by you. Please allow your child lots of practice attempts to learn to wash his or her hair and take a shower by himself or herself. Don't discourage your child by noticing only the mess that is left—praise the attempt!

Expect your child to wash his or her hands before eating, wash his or her face each night, and brush his or her teeth several times a day. We will be learning steps to complete these activities and will send home the list of steps. Please follow them carefully and help monitor his or her progress at home.

Thanks for your help!

Sincerely,

_____

Teacher

Skill Sheet #8: Progress Report

+ mastered
√ emerging
− not mastered

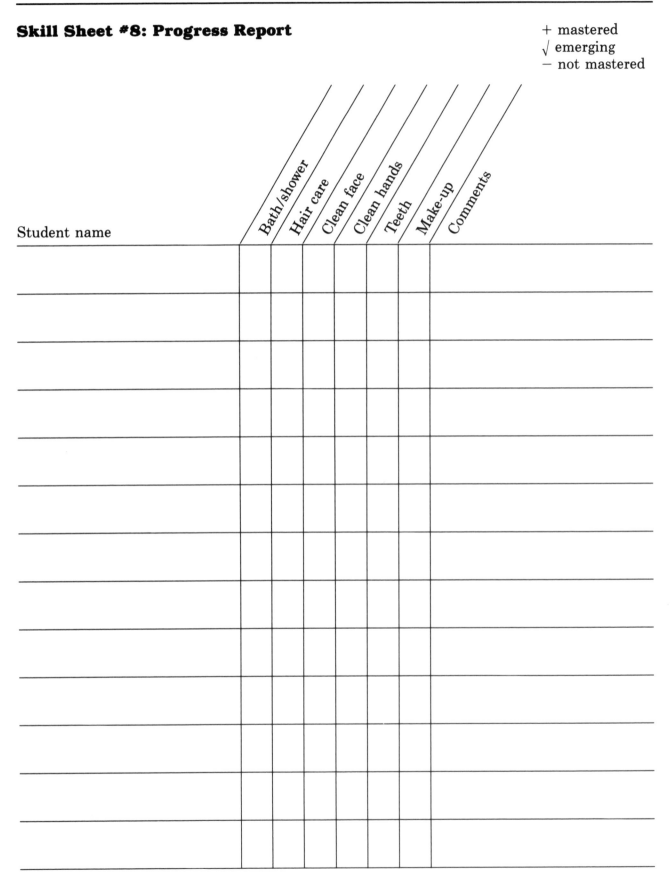

Student name	Bath/shower	Hair care	Clean face	Clean hands	Teeth	Make-up	Comments

TAKING A BATH OR SHOWER

Objective:

The student will state the appropriate sequential steps involved in taking a bath or shower.

Discussion:

Teacher: What do you do when your dog rolls in the mud or gets dirt all over? (bathe him) Why? (make him clean, look nice) Why do you think people take baths? (same reasons) It's very important for people to be clean. Some people take a bath or shower every single day. Who can tell me everything you need to gather up before you take a bath or shower? Let's make a list. (soap, towel, etc.) Now, let's make a list of everything you would need to do to take a good bath or shower.

Worksheet II-57 Carl is going to take a bath, but he got the list of instructions mixed up. The list is broken into four parts. Help Carl put the list in the correct order by numbering the parts 1 through 4 on the right side.

Answers:

2—1—4—3

Extension Activities:

1. **Magic Soap.** Have students write stories about taking a bath with magic soap that would turn them invisible, give magic powers, and so on. Leave the vocabulary words pertaining to baths on the board.

2. **Rub-a-dub-dub.** Have students practice adjusting the temperature on a bathtub faucet, draining the water, scrubbing out a bathtub ring, and so on. These sound like simple skills, but they are important for independence and courtesy to the next user.

TAKING A BATH OR SHOWER

Carl is planning to take a bath, but he got his directions all mixed up. The left side shows what he did and how he looks now. Put the steps in the correct order by numbering them on the right side.

get in the tub
rub soap and lather all over
scrub and rinse off soap

_____

get your washcloth, towel, soap and clean clothes
turn on the water
adjust the temperature
take off your clothes

_____

dry yourself off
put on clean clothes

_____

rinse off the soap
get out of the tub
drain the water

_____

HAIR CARE

Objective:

The student will state the appropriate sequential steps involved in maintaining clean hair.

Discussion:

Teacher: Part of looking your best has something to do with your hair. What do you think it is? (washing, brushing) No matter what style your hair is, it will look better if it is carefully taken care of. Some people wash their hair while they are in the shower; others wash it separately. However you do it, the steps are pretty much the same. First, let's list what supplies you'll need to get. (shampoo, creme rinse, towel, comb, dryer, etc.) Now, let's list the steps for washing your hair: (1) rinse, (2) shampoo, (3) rinse, (4) creme rinse (optional), (5) rinse. After your hair is clean and rinsed, then what should you do to take care of it? (style it, dry it, comb it)

Worksheet II-58 The students on this worksheet tried to take care of their hair but had problems. Write what you think is the problem on the line next to each situation. Then we'll discuss what you think each student should do to help take better care of his or her hair.

Answers:

1. Used too much shampoo/rinse it out
2. Left shampoo in hair/rinse it out
3. Didn't comb out hair/comb it
4. Left hair dryer on/turn it off
5. Dirty hair from not washing/wash it

Extension Activities:

1. **Way-out Hair.** Have students bring in pictures of exotic hair styles (punk rockers, weird styles, et cetera). Discuss the importance of hair and what people think of you. Do people notice hair styles?

2. **Makeover.** With parent permission, have a student volunteer for a hair makeover if you can arrange this with a local beauty salon. Have the stylist explain the finer points of taking care of your hair and ways to make it more attractive. Hearing her express the importance of healthy, clean hair will, it is hoped, make an impact on your students too.

HAIR CARE

These students did not follow the steps for caring for their hair. What mistakes did they make?

_____
_____
_____

_____
_____
_____

_____
_____
_____

_____
_____
_____

_____
_____
_____

A CLEAN FACE

Objective:

The student will state the appropriate sequential steps involved in washing and drying his or her face.

Discussion:

Teacher: We've talked about a clean body and clean hair. What's next? Another important part to take special care of is your face. Why do you think a clean face is important? (first thing people notice, etc.) Today we're going to talk about the steps for washing and drying your face and then go and practice!

Worksheet II-59 Here are some directions that this student is correctly following to wash and dry her face. Let's read over them and see if it makes sense; then we'll have a student volunteer come up and give it a try! When it's your turn, I'll help you check off each step that you can do correctly.

Extension Activities:

1. **Clown for a Day.** To give students a reason to wash their faces at school, have a clown theme for one day, allowing students to use special facial make-up to decorate themselves. (Or simple face painting on the cheeks may suffice.) At the end of the day or activity, take students to the rest room or sink area and have them wash their faces for you. You'll easily be able to tell which students need additional practice.

2. **Practice, Practice, Practice.** Enlist parents' help to encourage students to wash their faces at home and maintain a chart at school for one week, applying a sticker each day that the student successfully washes his or her face. At the end of the week, reward the student(s) with a small bar of soap!

II–59

A CLEAN FACE

Here are some directions for washing your face. Make sure you understand them and have everything you need. Put a checkmark after you have done each step correctly.

Step 1. Pull your hair out of the way. You might use a headband or rubber band if you have long hair.

 ☐

Step 2. Rinse all the surface dirt off your face with water.

 ☐

Step 3. Cover your hands with soap. Then apply the soap to your face. You might want to use special face soap.

 ☐

Step 4. Lather the soap all over your face in circular strokes. Really scrub!

 ☐

Step 5. Rinse all the soap off your face. You might want to use a clean washcloth for this.

 ☐

Step 6. Pat your face dry using your fingertips very gently or using a dry washcloth.

 ☐

Step 7. Put on a smile!

 ☐

TAKING CARE OF YOUR HANDS

Objective:

The student will state and demonstrate procedures for washing hands, keeping fingernails short and clean, and awareness of health/safety procedures involving germs or disease.

Discussion:

Teacher: What do you picture the hands of an old witch to look like? (warts, long nails) Now think about the hands of a doctor. (very clean) What do your hands tell about you? (hard-working, callouses, dirty, etc.) Why do you think it is important to have clean hands? (stop spread of germs, don't get things you touch dirty) What if the doctor was going to do surgery, but sneezed all over his hands before he started? It really is important to keep your hands clean, especially after you have touched something that may have germs on it. Can you give me any examples? (be prepared for unsavory answers) Today we're going to concentrate on ways to keep your hands clean and looking neat.

Worksheet II-60 These students have been given some rules about keeping hands clean. Read the situations and decide which rule each student needs to follow. Write your answer on the line next to each situation.

Answers:

1.	Rule 3	4.	Rule 4
2.	Rule 5	5.	Rule 2
3.	Rule 1	6.	Rule 5

Extension Activities:

1. **Achoo Posters.** Have each student draw his or her face from the front. Attach a tissue by the nose on the picture. Have students write a rule or message on each poster such as "When you sneeze, please use me!"

2. **Handwashing Practice.** Pretend you are a robot and have students give instructions as to how to wash your hands. Do not assume that you will use soap, for example, if they don't specify to "pick up the soap." Then let students work in pairs and practice giving good directions to each other. Inspect their hands.

TAKING CARE OF YOUR HANDS

These students are trying to follow the rules about keeping their hands clean and safe. Read what each student is saying, and then write the number of the rule that each is trying to follow.

Rule 1. Wash your hands with soap.

Rule 2. Dry your hands completely on a clean towel or cloth.

Rule 3. Keep your fingernails short.

Rule 4. Keep your fingernails clean.

Rule 5. Wash your hands if they are dirty or if you have touched something unhealthy.

1. Look at my hands! I'm going to use this fingernail file to make them look better! _____

2. Wow, it's fun playing with these old rusty tools! But now I better do something... _____

3. There, I've gotten water all over my hands. They're clean now, aren't they? _____

4. Why does my mom complain about this? Oh well, I'll take care of the problem. _____

5. I'll just wipe my wet hands on my pants, my pants that I've just been playing football in. _____

6. Aaaaachoooo! I know which rule I have to follow now! _____

CARE OF TEETH

Objective:

The student will brush his or her teeth in an appropriate manner and specify at least one purpose for visiting the dentist.

Discussion:

Teacher: What would happen to me if I never brushed my teeth? (rotten teeth, bad breath) I'll bet every one of you did something to your teeth this morning. What was it? (brushed them) Tell me the name of the person who helps you take care of your teeth—what is he or she called? (dentist) Well, if you can brush your own teeth, why should you visit a dentist? (he can find cavities, pull teeth, correct teeth, etc.) Why do you think it is recommended to visit a dentist twice a year? (cavity prevention, takes several months for cavity to form)

Worksheet II-61 Today you are going to follow a girl, Flossie, as she takes care of her teeth. There are words missing from each part. Write the missing words on the lines supplied; then put the circled letters in order to form a word that has something to do with good dental care.

Answers:

1. Brush
2. Miss
3. Rinse
4. Floss
5. Dentist.
   Word: Smile

Extension Activities:

1. **Visit from "Jaws".** Have a dentist, if possible, bring and explain current proper dental brushing procedures by using a model of a human jaw with teeth intact. If a dentist is not available, literature and a model can usually be obtained from your local dental society or dentist. A school nurse may also be able to help with this.

2. **A Tooth Speaks.** Have students pretend they are a tooth in their own mouth. Have the tooth describe what it feels like to be brushed, flossed, and possibly have a cavity forming.

CARE OF TEETH

Flossie is taking good care of her teeth. Follow her through the day as she shows you what she is doing. Write the missing word on each line next to the pictures. Then, at the end, put the circled letters in order at the bottom to spell out a good word for you to remember to show off good dental care.

1. Flossie gets up in the morning and pulls out her green tooth __ __ __◯__.

2. Then she puts toothpaste on the toothbrush and moves the brush up and down all over her teeth. She is careful not to◯__ __ __ any spots; she gets them all!

3. After the toothpaste is scrubbed all over her teeth, she uses clean water to __◯__ __ __out the tooth-paste. She spits it into the sink and lets it drain.

4. Now she gets the dental floss and uses the string to get out any little bits of food that may be left or caught in between her teeth. Flossie thinks that __◯__ __-ing is fun!

5. It's time for Flossie to visit the lady who can help her check for cavities and give her teeth an excellent cleaning. This person is Flossie's __◯__ __ __ __ __.

Now put the circled letters in order. How can you show off your good dental care?

___ ___ ___ ___ ___

MAKE-UP

Objective:

The student will state when use of make-up is appropriate.

Discussion:

Teacher: Pretend you're getting ready to go out trick-or-treating for Halloween. You are dressed as a little green creature from Mars. What might you do to your face? (use green make-up) Now pretend you're going as an Indian from the Old West days. How might your face look? (stripes, war paint) How would wearing make-up change your appearance? (make people look at you, cover or hide your own face) Why do you think people wear make-up today for ordinary use? (cover up blemishes or wrinkles, look attractive) Lots of people, especially women and girls, like to wear make-up because they feel that it makes them look more attractive by covering up any blemishes they may have or adding colors to have attention drawn to them. But what kind of attention would I have drawn to me if I came to school looking like a strange creature or with war paint on my face? (people would laugh, think you look odd) When you use make-up, make sure that you use it to make yourself more attractive, not to get attention for looking weird. Can anyone give me examples of too much make-up? (models in magazines, fluorescent eye shadow, et cetera)

Worksheet II-62 These students are using make-up, but some of them are not thinking where they are or how much make-up they should be using to look attractive. Write Yes or No if you think each is using make-up appropriately or not.

Answers:

1. No (bad taste)   5. No
2. Yes   6. Yes
3. No   7. No
4. Yes

Extension Activities:

1. **How Much Is Too Much?** Have students page through magazines (particularly women's magazines) and discuss what products are shown that will make someone attractive. What about overdoing perfume? Or clothing? Or hair styles? Have students select pictures of people whom they think are quite attractive and discuss what features about them are interesting, unusual, or noticed.

2. **Makeover.** If you can get a cosmetologist to visit your class, have her take the girls aside and show them ways to use make-up to enhance their looks. Let the girls practice putting on make-up with each other and then make a "grand entrance" into the room. Take pictures—before and after. Emphasize that there is a happy medium to using cosmetics. (Some girls can benefit from using make-up just to make themselves feel pretty and by spending a little extra time taking care of themselves. Other girls may need to reduce the amount they use, mistakingly thinking that "more is better.")

Name _____ Date _____

II–62

MAKE-UP

These students are using make-up for different reasons. Tell if you think each student is using make-up appropriately. Write *yes* or *no* on the lines.

1. _____ I'm going to a funeral, so I'm going to paint my fingernails black and use black eyeshadow and black lipstick.

2. _____ I've got a pimple on my cheek. A little bit of this make-up should cover it up and maybe even help it heal.

3. _____ I want to look like I'm tan, so I'm going to put a ton of this dark make-up all over my face.

4. _____ I'm so pale—a little of this blush will make me look healthy.

5. _____ People will notice my pretty blue eyes if I use my eyeliner to make designs!!

6. _____ My face has darker spots in places—this facial cover-up will even that out.

7. _____ I'm going swimming for P.E. first hour—but I'll just put all this make-up back on in the restroom after that class.

Dear Parents,

If your child is to learn to become independent, he or she needs to learn to maintain a clean room, whether it is shared with a brother or sister, used as a toyroom/study/gymnasium/video room, or kept under lock and key with no visitors allowed. At some point in life, we all must face the fact that if we don't do it, nobody else will.

Most children will accept the responsibility of keeping their room picked up if they are taught specifically how to do it and are checked on occasionally to make sure that their standards haven't dropped. ("No, dishes under the bed are *not* considered to be put away.") Make your expectations very clear— what specifically do you want them to do? Follow through on your consequences— if the room is not up to your standards, what's your alternative?

During this unit, please allow your child to participate in the joys of cleaning up! Show him or her where the cleaning supplies are kept, how much to use, and how you want the task completed. Don't forget to praise the efforts as much as the outcome!

Sincerely,

_____

Teacher

Skill Sheet #9: Progress Report

+ mastered
√ emerging
− not mastered

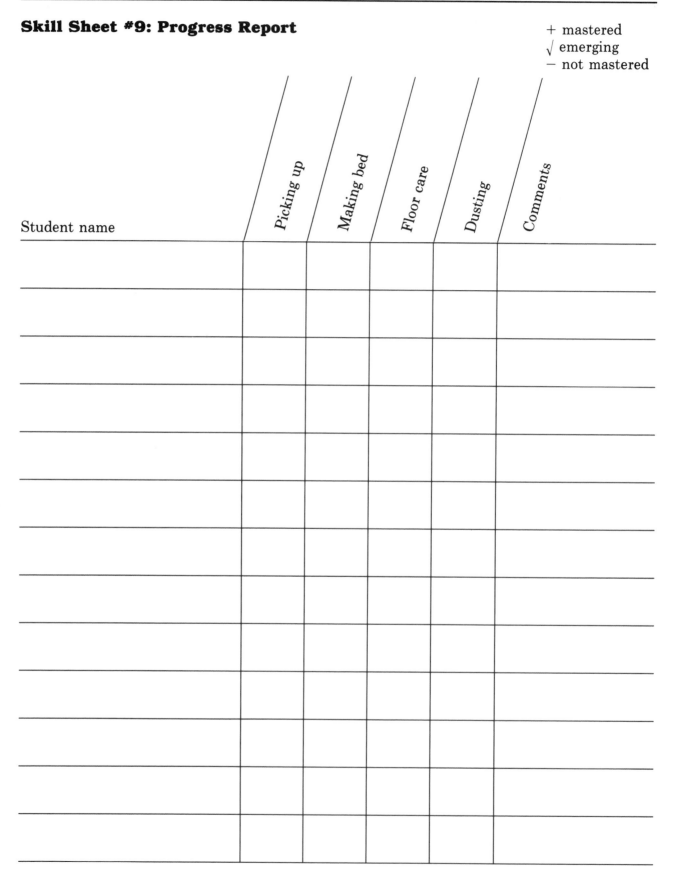

Student name	Picking up	Making bed	Floor care	Dusting	Comments

PICKING UP

Objective:

The student will participate in keeping his or her room clean by picking up all items from the floor or other places where they do not belong and placing the items in an appropriate place.

Discussion:

Teacher: Think about your room at home. Now describe what it looks like. (messy, organized, specific items) Today we're going to be talking about picking up your room. What does that mean? (put things where they belong) What kinds of things do you usually leave lying around in your room?

Worksheet II-63 Dennis the Disorganized is a student who needs some help returning items all over his room to their appropriate spot. Help him by matching the things that need to be picked up with the place that each should go.

Answers:

1. b	6. h
2. d	7. e
3. f	8. i
4. g	9. a
5. j	10. c

Extension Activities:

1. **A Peek in Your Room.** Have students use construction paper to make a large door (complete with door knob and signs or stickers that may be on their door). Arrange it so that the door can be "opened" with paper underneath. Have students draw what a visitor might find if they made a surprise visit to their room. (If students share a room with a sibling or someone else, they could include that person's belongings also.)

2. **Clean-up Math.** Have students write story problems involving items that are usually associated with having to be picked up. Exchange problems and have students solve them. (Example: George had three dirty plates in his room, each with four pieces of pizza on them. How many pieces of pizza were there in all?) Pictures are also welcomed!

_____

PICKING UP
_____

Dennis the Disorganized was told by his father to "pick up the room." Help him match the item with the proper place. Write the letter of the place next to each item.

_____ 1. A dirty shirt

_____ 2. A clean shirt

_____ 3. A shoe

_____ 4. A pencil

_____ 5. A towel

_____ 6. School books

_____ 7. A bike tire

_____ 8. Skateboard magazines

_____ 9. A pop can

_____ 10. A plate with cold pizza on it from last week's dinner

a. In the recycling bag in the garage

b. In the dirty laundry bucket

c. To the dishwasher (after dumping out the food in the kitchen trash)

d. On a hanger in his closet

e. On his bike in the garage

f. Next to the other shoe on the floor of his closet

g. In the pencil can on his desk

h. Stacked neatly on his desk

i. In a magazine rack next to his desk

j. In the bathroom

MAKING THE BED

Objective:

The student will follow appropriate steps to make a bed, including changing sheets, pillows, and bedspread.

Discussion:

Teacher: Does this ever happen at your house? You find out that a guest is coming, and your mom or dad says that you have to help get the guest bed ready? What has to be done? (prepare a nice-looking bed) What's involved in making a bed? (flat sheets, blanket neatly tucked in, pillow in place, bedspread smoothed-out) Why do you think a neat-looking bed is important? What if nobody ever comes in your room to see it anyway? (A good point! Stress that even if no one sees it, it's a good skill to know how to prepare a bed for visitors.)

Worksheet II-64 There are probably lots of different ways to make a bed. Some people just throw the blankets on; others take special care for each and every step. This worksheet shows a step-by-step way that you could make your bed. Even if this is not the way you normally do it, let's go through the steps and make sure that you understand at least one way to do it. (You may want to send this sheet home as an assignment. Have a parent go through it with the student and initial it when completed.)

Extension Activities:

1. **I Did It Chart.** Continue a cooperative effort with parents at home to monitor and reward bed-making behavior. Encourage parents to let their child work on this task (even though it may be easier for the parent to do it instead at first).

2. **Step-by-Step Photos.** If you have access to a practice bed at school, use a camera to photograph students in various steps of the bed-making procedure. Have students arrange the pictures in sequential order on a poster and verbally explain what is involved in each step.

MAKING THE BED

Here are some directions for making a bed. Make sure you understand each step. Put a checkmark next to each step after you have completed it correctly.

Step 1. Put the bottom sheet neatly on the bed. Make sure it is centered and tucked in.

Step 2. Put the top sheet over the bed. Fold back the top edge a little bit.

Step 3. Now put the blanket on top of the top sheet. Fold the top edge back.

Step 4. Put the pillow or pillows at the head of the bed. Fluff them up!

Step 5. Now you might want to tuck in the blanket and sheet all around the bed. Don't make it too tight or you'll have trouble getting in!

Step 6. If you use a bedspread, put that over every-thing and take extra care to tuck in part of it under the pillow. Then bring the top up to the head of the bed.

Step 7. You might want to put a stuffed animal on top!

FLOOR CARE

Objective:

The student will specify what cleaning activity is most appropriate for the floor in his or her room (vacuuming, sweeping) and follow appropriate steps to clean the floor.

Discussion:

Teacher: Look at our floor. Does anyone know how it is cleaned? (vacuumed, swept) Part of keeping your room clean is making sure that the floor is clean. Why do you think the floor gets dirty? (shoes left on, walked on, stuff thrown on the floor) Basically, there are two ways to clean a floor. If you have carpeting, you can vacuum it. If you have a hard floor, you can mop it and sweep it to keep it clean. Today we're going to learn how the different ways help keep the floor clean.

Worksheet II-65 This worksheet shows some tools that can help keep a floor clean. On the first part, you will match the name of the tool with the picture of it. On the second part, use the names from the top to complete the paragraphs of students explaining how they keep their floor clean.

Answers:

a. 2		Story
b. 3		1. vacuum cleaner
c. 1		2. broom, dustpan
d. 2		3. mop, bucket, bucket
e. 3		

Extension Activities:

1. **Cleaning Extravaganza.** Have students collect pictures of different cleaning products. Categorize them into various functions, rooms they could be used in, types of procedures (mopping, dusting, etc.).

2. **Floor Inventory.** Have students complete a simple chart indicating the type of floor surface in the various rooms of their home. Discuss why many kitchens are not carpeted or why people may use small rugs in certain areas or rooms.

FLOOR CARE

These students are using different materials to clean their floors. Match each material with the method used. 1 = vacuuming 2 = mopping 3 = sweeping

a. Bucket _____

b. Broom _____

c. Vacuum cleaner _____

d. Mop _____

e. Dustpan _____

Now use the words above to complete the cleaning stories below.

1. My room is carpeted, so I am going to get the _____ _____. I will plug it in to the socket on the wall, turn it on, and move it all around the floor to pick up the dirt.

2. My floor is not too dirty, so I am going to get a long _____ and sweep all of the dirt from the corners and even under the bed into the center. Then I'll use the _____ to collect the dirt, and I'll dump it out.

3. My room is really dirty today, so I'm going to get a _____ and put it in this _____ of soapy water. Then I'll move it back and forth all over the floor, rinsing it out in the _____ every once in a while. I'll let it dry — and it'll be nice and clean again!

© 1992 by The Center for Applied Research in Education

DUSTING

Objective:

The student will dust a designated area with proper materials and in a safe and thorough manner.

Discussion:

Teacher: Achooo! There must be some dust in this room! Since we've been talking about keeping rooms clean, what do you think might need to be done to get rid of dust? (dusting, cleaning dirt in the air) What is dust, anyway? (small particles of dirt or matter in the air) How could we get rid of it? (feather duster, fan, spray cleaner) What happens when a lot of dust settles on something? (covers with fine layer) What commercials have you seen that involve cleaning to get rid of dust? (writing name on table, etc.) Does anyone know some good materials to eliminate dust? (rag, dusters, commercial sprays)

Worksheet II-66 The students on this worksheet have been asked to dust, but only one is dusting in a manner that is going to get the job done properly. Circle the student who is dusting properly. Then we will discuss what the others are doing wrong.

Answers:

1. Ineffective way to remove dust and probably unappreciated by neighbor
2. Too much spray
3. Didn't dust at all
4. Deodorant doesn't substitute for spray cleaner
5. Good job
6. Broom is too large for small expensive knickknack cleaning.

Extension Activities:

1. **Dust in the Room.** Have students focus on one room at a time and try to come up with five to ten places where they might find dust. Then take a look to see if they were right. Which rooms tend to be dustier? Why?

2. **Room Dusters.** Have students take turns being the room duster. Supply a colorful hang duster, clean rags, and spray, if desired. Be sure to evaluate the job done.

DUSTING

Only one student below is dusting the right way. The others are doing at least one thing wrong. Circle the student who is doing a good job and explain why the others are not doing a good job.

1. I'll get rid of that dust! I'll blow it all at my neighbor's house!

2. There, that should take care of the dust on that table!

3. No one will see the dust on top of the bookshelf, so I'll consider this job done!

4. I'll use this spray deodorant to clean off the top of this table. It looks just about like the spray stuff Mom uses when she dusts.

5. First, I'll spray this on the table, then I'll carefully wipe it with a clean rag until there aren't anymore streaks.

6. I can use this broom to dust the knickknacks on this shelf. I'll be careful since they are very, very valuable.

Dear Parents,

Our next group of lessons centers on obtaining food, preparing it for eating, and cleaning up afterward. There are several ways that you can help reinforce these lessons at home.

Let your child help you when you shop for food. If you tend to shop at the same store, let your child become familiar with various locations of items and send him or her to help you retrieve them. Direct your child's attention to notice what items are grouped together in the store.

In the kitchen, let your child become involved in simple steps of preparing a meal. Let him or her see the entire process and assist you whenever possible on some of the steps. Don't forget to have your child help in cleaning up the dishes afterward!

Thanks again for helping with the home-school bridge of communication!

Sincerely,

_____

Teacher

Skill Sheet #10: Progress Report

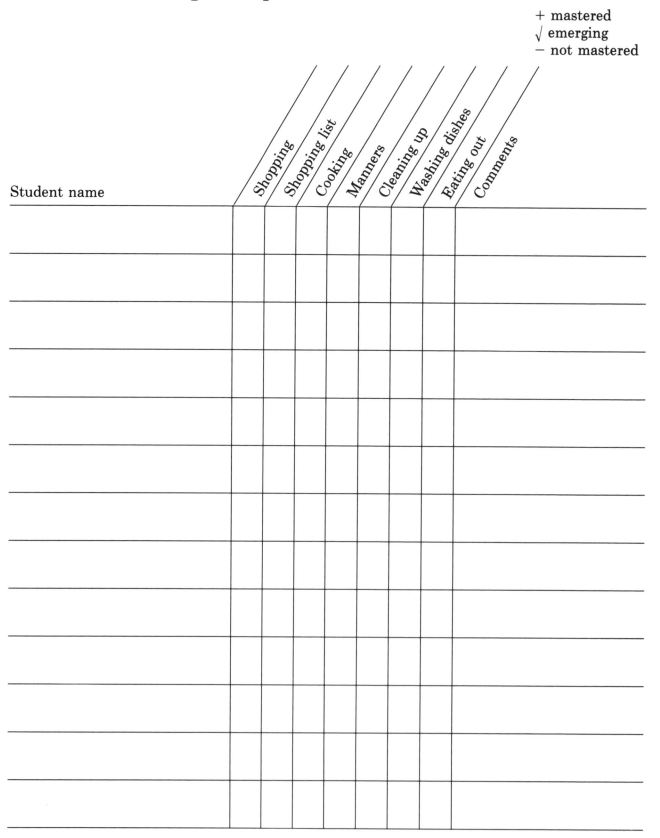

+ mastered
√ emerging
− not mastered

Shopping | Shopping list | Cooking | Manners | Cleaning up | Washing dishes | Eating out | Comments

Student name

SHOPPING FOR FOOD

Objective:

The student will identify numerous items of food that can be obtained at a local grocery store.

Discussion:

Teacher: I'm hungry. Is anybody else hungry? If we wanted to prepare a nice meal, where could we get the things we need? (grocery store) Who can help me list 20 things you can buy at the grocery store to help you with a meal? (specify if you want to include nonfood items, such as napkins, paper plates, etc.) Most grocery stores now carry all kinds of nonfood items too. Can you list ten? (games, cards, videos, toys)

Worksheet II-67 Here is a list of items that can be found in a grocery store. When you do this activity, I want you to check off each item that you found and write down what row or aisle or section you found it in. We'll see if there's a pattern in different stores.

Discuss with students why certain items may be grouped together, stored in refrigerators/freezers, or sold fresh.

Extension Activities:

1. **Food Hunt.** When planning a school party, you may be able to take students shopping for needed items. Have students pair up and locate various items. This activity is not a race, but should be carried out systematically. Instead of wandering all around the store, have students think about where it would most likely be found.

2. **Store Map.** If possible, have students draw a general map of the local grocery store, indicating where various items are located. Have them walk slowly around the store and come up with general categories ("vegetables" instead of "corn, beans, peas", etc.).

SHOPPING FOR FOOD

Here is a list of items commonly found in any grocery store. Check off each one as you find it, and write down the location (row, aisle, etc.).

Item	✔	Where
1. Frozen green beans		
2. Can of corn		
3. Fresh carrots		
4. Box of cookies		
5. Tomato soup in a can		
6. Loaf of bread		
7. Frozen dinner		
8. Fresh hamburger		
9. Gallon of milk		
10. Box of cereal		
11. Paper plates		
12. Canned pop		
13. Potato chips		
14. Bacon		
15. Brownie mix		

© 1992 by The Center for Applied Research in Education

MAKING A SHOPPING LIST

Objective:

Given a situation or meal, the student will make a list of needed items.

Discussion:

Teacher: Would it be fun to have a class party for another class/your parents/your pen pals/class volunteers, and so on? What would happen if I dropped you all off at the door of the store and said, "Get what we need!" (duplicate items, chaos in the store, run out of money) What would be a good way to make sure none of that happened? (make a list, be sure you have enough money before you start) Would you need the same things if you were having friends over for dinner as you would if you were having people you didn't know over for snacks? Would you have to think about how many people were coming over too?

Worksheet II-68 Help these students make lists of things that they need at a grocery store. Then we will talk about what things you all felt were important. Do you think everyone's list will be exactly the same?

Answers: (examples)

1. Snacks (popcorn, soda)
2. Cake, ice cream, napkins, plates, balloons
3. Pizza mix, soda, garlic bread
4. Potato chips, popcorn, cookies, vegetables, and dip

Extension Activities:

1. **Class Party.** Begin planning an "event" that your class could host for another group. Have students make invitations, plan activities, and make a list of needed items. Really promote this.

2. **Helping at Home.** When parents need items at the store, have the students find the needed things on the list. Parents may want to divide their shopping list so that the student can get items located in a certain area, items that the student is likely to need, and so on. The sooner the student is familiar with the store, the more help he or she can be to the parent shopper.

Name _____   Date _____

II–68

MAKING A SHOPPING LIST

These students are going to have a party or special event at their house. Help each make a list of needed items. Write your answers on the lines.

1. Ronald is having friends over to watch a basketball game at his house after dinner.

   _____

   _____

   _____

2. Sandy is having a birthday party in the afternoon for a few friends.

   _____

   _____

   _____

3. Alex wants to make pizza for dinner for his family.

   _____

   _____

   _____

   _____

4. Kim is having a swimming party all day at her house and wants to have snacks for people to munch on.

   _____

   _____

   _____

   _____

SIMPLE COOKING, EASY MEALS

Objective:

The student will follow directions for preparing a meal or particular part of a meal.

Discussion:

Teacher: If I came over to your house and said that I'd like something to eat, what could you fix for me? What if I expected to stay for a whole meal? What would you like me to have? How would you prepare a dish if you weren't sure? (ask someone, use a cookbook or recipe) Today we're going to learn about preparing simple things to eat. By "simple," I mean just a few steps to follow. Can anyone name some things that are easy to prepare?(sandwich, soup, etc.)

Worksheet II-69 Would you like to try cooking something? Here is a list of some foods that can be prepared quite easily. Your job is to find out how to do that. Then we'll compare our answers and give it a try!

Answers: (examples)

Have students list all materials that need to be gathered
List sequential steps for preparing the item (turn on the oven, cut up the fruit, flip the hamburger over, etc.)
Explain how the ingredients are combined

Extension Activities:

1. **Chef for a Day.** Have students try out a simple recipe at home, perhaps using something that their parents often serve or enjoy eating. They could tell about their experience and how it turned out— perhaps even bring in a bit of their homework.

2. **Class Cookbook.** Have each student bring in or contribute one simple recipe or procedure for preparing one item of food. Combine the directions into a class cookbook. Have students illustrate the steps and the final product. You may want to reproduce enough copies for each student to have his or her own.

SIMPLE COOKING, EASY MEALS

Here are some items that are fairly easy to prepare or cook. Find out the different steps involved in each and list them below. Circle one food item that you would like to try to make.

1. Peanut butter and jelly sandwich _____
   _____
   _____

2. Chicken noodle soup from a can _____
   _____
   _____

3. A cup of hot chocolate _____
   _____
   _____

4. Brownies from a mix _____
   _____
   _____
   _____

5. Fresh fruit salad _____
   _____
   _____

6. Hamburger patty (on a stove) _____
   _____
   _____

7. Macaroni and cheese from a mix _____
   _____
   _____

8. A frozen TV dinner _____
   _____
   _____

TABLE MANNERS

Objective:

The student will demonstrate courteous table behavior when eating socially.

Discussion:

Teacher: Who can describe for me what the lunchroom is like? Is it noisy, fun, or what? Why do people have to stand in line to get a hot lunch? (orderly) When you eat food or meals with other people, there are certain things that you should do to show that you have good manners at the table. What are some of the lunchroom rules that help make things orderly or show good manners? (keep noise level down, don't all run for hot lunch at once, etc.) Why do you think it's important to have good table manners?

Worksheet II-70 Every home has its own set of rules or table manners. Here are some examples of students either following or not following a table rule. Circle the students who are showing good table manners; X the students who are not.

Answers:

1. X, O
2. O, X
3. O, X
4. X, O

Extension Activities:

1. **At Our House. . . .** Have students draw an outline of a house and write a rule that is important for good table manners at *their* house (guests eat first, pray before eating, wash hands, etc.). Discuss why each rule is important.

2. **Party Time!** Have an event for which your students can play the part of "host" or "hostess" for visitors. Rehearse polite phrases ("Thank you for coming," "I hope you enjoyed it," "Would you like another brownie?" etc.) and actions (give everyone a napkin, make sure everyone has a nametag). This might also be a good opportunity to practice getting all cleaned up! Students will love getting compliments on their excellent manners. (Be sure to inform guests that the students are demonstrating good manners!)

TABLE MANNERS

Here are some examples of table manners. Circle the student in each pair who is showing good manners; put an X on the student who is not.

1. Wait until everyone at your table has his or her food before you start eating if you are sharing food.

2. Share the food with everyone.

3. Pass food politely.

4. Have nice topics of conversation at the table.

CLEANING UP

Objective:

The student will specify the proper procedure for handling leftovers, removing dishes and tableware from the table, and cleaning up the eating area.

Discussion:

Teacher: What happens after you've eaten a meal at home? (leave, clean up) What happens here at school when your lunch time is over? (throw trash away, line up to leave lunchroom) Since there's a proper procedure for everything else connected with eating and food, do you think there might be good things to do after you eat a meal to help clean up the area? What things need to be taken care of? (dishes, leftovers, crumbs)

Worksheet II-71 Here is a story about a mixed-up girl who is trying to clean up. She made a few mistakes, however. Put an X on the pictures that show where her mistake is.

Answers:

1. Closet/dishwasher
2. Blankets and towels/aluminum foil or plastic wrap
3. Bag/trash or garbage disposal
4. Vacuum cleaner/paper towel or dishrag

Extension Activities:

1. **Cafeteria Helpers.** Some schools allow students to help clean up in the cafeteria after meals in return for cookies, reduced rates on meals, or simply for vocational training. Often students enjoy being able and allowed to do this activity. It should not be perceived as a demeaning job; rather, view it as a vocational training task.

2. **Behind-the-Scenes at McDonald's.** McDonald's and other fast-food restaurants sometimes offer tours of the facilities to school groups. If you can, arrange for your students to hear about the standards of cleanliness required by many restaurants, specifically what happens to leftovers and trash. Does your community recycle? Do your local restaurants participate?

Name _____   Date _____

II–71

CLEANING UP

Molly is mixed up today. She is trying to clean up after a meal at her home, but she has one thing wrong in everything she is doing. Put an X on her mistake and write a better choice on the line next to each picture.

1. Everyone has finished eating, so Molly decided to take the plates, glasses, and silverware and put them in the closet so they would come out clean.

 _____

2. Molly took the leftover food and wrapped up the food that she wanted to save. She put blankets and towels around the food and put them in the refrigerator.

 _____

3. Some of the food was not worth saving. Molly scraped the food off of the plates and threw it into a bag that had her homework in it.

 _____

4. There were crumbs and water drops on the table, so Molly got a vacuum cleaner and wiped them up. Then she threw them into the trash.

 _____

WASHING THE DISHES

Objective:

The student will demonstrate ability to wash, rinse, and dry tableware manually.

Discussion:

Teacher: We already talked about cleaning up after you have a meal, but there's one task that we didn't talk about. It has to do with cleaning up the dishes. Can anyone think of it? (washing the dishes) Why can't you just brush off the food and put the dishes back? (soap gets rid of any germs; promotes better health, sanitation) Today we're going to work on washing dishes—and that includes glasses, bowls, and silverware.

Worksheet II-72 Here are the steps for one way to learn to wash dishes. Remember, you might wash them differently at home, so the directions may not be exactly the same as you have heard before. That's all right—the important thing is that you learn at least one good method! When you work on this at home, be sure to have someone watch you to make sure you are doing it correctly. Then check off each step.

Extension Activities:

1. **Kitchen Coupons.** Have students devise a "coupon book" containing coupons good for one washing of dishes. Have the students make several kinds—perhaps one would be good for breakfast dishes, another for Sunday dinner, and so on, depending on the family life-style. Have parents redeem the coupons from the student. Require signatures and a comment from the parent on the back of the coupon.

2. **Kitchen Assistant.** For students who may not be totally competent to wash dishes independently, assign only one or a few steps to be learned and demonstrated. Students may enjoy helping a parent or sibling with the dish washing process, yet not be entirely responsible for the complete task.

II–72

WASHING THE DISHES

Here are some steps for washing dishes. Put a checkmark next ✔ to each step after you understand it and have completed it correctly.

Step 1. Fill the sink with hot water. Squirt in some dish detergent as you fill the sink.

Step 2. Put the dishes, glasses, and silverware into the sink. Let them soak for a few minutes to loosen any food particles.

Step 3. Use a scrubbing pad or cloth to go over the dishes to make sure all of the food particles are off.

Step 4. Rinse the dishes. Be sure to get off all the soap!

Step 5. Dry them with a clean towel or let them drip dry.

Step 6. Drain the water and clean out the sink.

EATING OUT

Objective:

The student will state the usual sequential steps involved in obtaining a meal at a restaurant, including seating, ordering, paying the bill, and tipping.

Discussion:

Teacher: I'll bet all of you have had a meal recently that was not cooked by someone at your house or at a friend's house. Where else can you get food? (school cafeteria, restaurant, fast-food restaurant, convenience store) What's different about eating at a restaurant from eating at someone's house? (pay for it, are served, food may taste better/worse) Eating out is fun to do, isn't it? Where are your favorite places to eat out, when you have the chance?

Worksheet II-73 Randy is a student who eats some of his meals at home and sometimes eats out. You are to read over the sentences that tell about Randy and decide if he is eating at home or out. Write the words *home* or *out* on the lines next to each picture.

Answers:

1. Home, out	3. Home, out
2. Out, home	4. Home, out

Extension Activities

1. **Menu Math.** Collect menus from some local restaurants. Have students practice being the customers and role play the process of entering the restaurant, ordering from the menu, and paying for the bill. You may want to incorporate math skills, calculator skills, and reading skills into this activity. Students may want to be the hostess or waitperson in this role play also.

2. **My Favorite Restaurant.** Survey students as to their favorite fast-food restaurant, item (french fries, chicken, dessert), or slogan. Combine responses and make a large graph. Also include containers with restaurant logos or ads to brighten up the graph. You could also survey students as to how often they eat out, how often they go to a particular fast-food place, or how many french fries a particular place includes in a regular order.

EATING OUT

Randy ate one meal at home and another meal in a restaurant. Look at each set of pictures. Write *home* if it took place at Randy's home; write *out* if it took place when he ate out. Write your answers on the lines next to the pictures.

1. Randy went to the table and sat down.
   _____

Randy waited for the lady to tell him where to sit. _____

2. Randy looked through the menu to pick out what he wanted to eat. _____

Randy passed the dishes around the table and put some of everything on his plate. _____

3. Randy politely passed what other people wanted and waited until everyone was finished to leave the table.

   _____

Randy politely passed what other people wanted and waited until the waiter gave them a bill before he got up.

   _____

4. Randy helped clear off the table and washed the dishes. _____

Randy gave the cashier some money and left some on the table for a tip.

   _____

© 1992 by The Center for Applied Research in Education

Dear Parents,

Teaching a child to eat properly, seek medical attention when necessary, and get enough exercise seem to be fairly obvious bits of advice. But children sometimes need specific teaching and lessons at home to truly value taking care of himself or herself as a priority. Do you engage in leisure activities that your child could take part in? Are there healthy family activities that all would enjoy?

These lessons deal with "doing the right thing," as far as health habits are concerned. But probably the best lesson that your child will receive is that of watching you engage in healthful living. At home, emphasize good living habits by being a good example.

Thanks!

Sincerely,

_____

Teacher

Skill Sheet #11: Progress Report

+ mastered
√ emerging
− not mastered

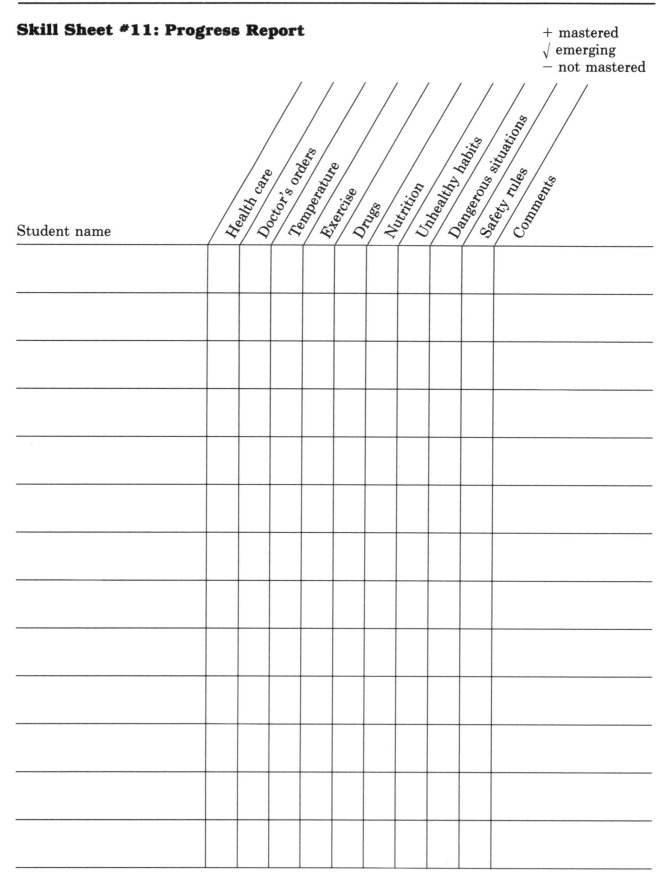

Student name	Health care	Doctor's orders	Temperature	Exercise	Drugs	Nutrition	Unhealthy habits	Dangerous situations	Safety rules	Comments

VISITING HEALTH CARE PEOPLE

Objective:

The student will state the importance of and purpose for visiting health care professionals.

Discussion:

Teacher: During the next few weeks we'll be talking about ways to keep yourself healthy and safe. Why do you think that's important? (live longer, live better) I'll bet you can think of some people whose job it is to help you stay healthy. (doctor, pharmacist, nurse, dentist) Why don't those people come to your house to take care of you? (don't know when you're sick, have offices to take care of many people) So whose job is it to make sure you get to see someone when you need help? (parents, student) What could happen if you had a health problem and didn't do anything about it? (might get worse)

Worksheet II-74 These students have some health problems and need to see someone who can help them. Match the student with the person who could best help him or her. Write the letter next to each student.

Answers:

1. b	4. c
2. f	5. a
3. d	6. e

Extension Activities:

1. **Doctor, Doctor.** As a vocabulary-building exercise, list some of the many specialties that doctors in your area practice. Common ones may include dermatology, ophthalmology, pediatrics, radiology, and anesthesiology. Students may have had experience in visiting one or more of these doctors.

2. **Health in the News.** Have students begin collecting magazine or newspaper articles dealing with health issues. Design a bulletin board that highlights "health in the news." Discuss vocabulary such as "cholesterol," "blood pressure," and "vaccination."

VISITING HEALTH CARE PEOPLE

These students have some health needs. Match the student with the health care person who could help him. Write the letter next to each student.

_____ 1. John can't see the board in his classroom very well. Sometimes things look very blurry to him.

           a. Doctor

           b. Eye doctor

_____ 2. Amy fell on the playground and cut her arm. It is bleeding a little bit.

           c. Dentist

_____ 3. Sylvia needs to take medication for her allergies. If she doesn't, she feels very sick.

           d. Pharmacist

_____ 4. Josh has a big tooth growing in his mouth, but the small tooth hasn't fallen out yet. Sometimes his teeth hurt.

           e. X-ray technician

_____ 5. Mario needs to have a physical before he can play on the school football team.

           f. Nurse (school nurse)

_____ 6. Ben had an operation on his leg and has to have X rays taken every two weeks.

FOLLOWING DOCTOR'S ORDERS

Objective:

The student will identify whether or not an order from a doctor has been followed correctly.

Discussion:

Teacher: Sometimes when you visit a doctor, you leave with a little piece of paper that gives you directions for how to take your medicine or just what you should do to get better. Does anyone know what that is called? (prescription) A *prescription* is a written direction that you should follow to get better or stay healthy. Sometimes you may not get a prescription, but the doctor will tell you something such as "stay in bed, get plenty of rest," or "take two aspirin and call me in the morning." Have any of you ever had a prescription or directions to follow after you've visited a doctor?

Worksheet II-75 These students were given orders to follow from their doctors. One in each case is following the instructions; the other is not. Circle the one who is following orders.

Answers:

1. Second
2. First
3. First
4. Second

Extension Activities:

1. **Prescriptions for a Good Day.** Have students write a "prescription" for what would give them a good day; for example, "say two nice things to someone," or "start your day with a big candy bar," and so on. Add a huge adhesive bandage and display their thoughts in the hallway.

2. **Why?** Discuss reasons why a doctor may prescribe a certain activity (or restriction). Students may not be aware that in some cases a pill should be taken several days *after* the symptoms disappear in order to be effective. Bed rest may not feel good, but may be necessary for the body to restore itself. Prescription drugs can have different effects on different people because of size, age, and body chemistry. Discuss these and other situations.

FOLLOWING DOCTOR'S ORDERS

These students were given orders from their doctor. One in each situation is following the doctor's orders. The other is not. Circle the one who is correctly following instructions.

1. "Take one pill every four hours."

2. "Do not take this medication with any other medication."

3. "Don't take anyone else's medication."

4. "Get plenty of rest."

TAKING YOUR TEMPERATURE

Objective:

The student will identify a normal temperature reading and use a thermometer to take his temperature accurately.

Discussion:

Teacher: Have you ever felt this way: your head hurts, your forehead is really hot, and you feel like you're burning up? What is that called? (death's door, fever, really sick) A *fever* is when your body temperature is above normal. Does anyone know what your normal temperature is? (98.6 degrees) If your temperature is a few degrees above that, you will probably feel hot and sick. A fever can be good because it means your body is fighting off the condition that is weakening your body. Often a doctor will want to know your body temperature to help him or her decide how to help you get better. Today we're going to work on taking your temperature. (You may want to recruit the school nurse to assist with thermometer distribution and disinfecting.)

Worksheet II-76 Have students follow the directions to practice taking their temperature and check off each step as it is correctly completed. Since most students will probably have a normal reading, be sure to complete the exercises on the bottom of the sheet.

Answers:

- a. 100.3 degrees
- b. 98.2 degrees
- c. 98.7 degrees
- d. 101.5 degrees

Extension Activities:

1. **Jumbo Thermometer:** Students may have trouble distinguishing between the different degrees on a small thermometer. Use a large bulletin board or wall space to create a very large paper thermometer with degree marks clearly marked. You may want to devise a red strip of paper or thick yarn to represent the mercury in the thermometer and demonstrate how it fluctuates by moving it up and down. Ask students to show you where 98.6 degrees is on the thermometer and mark it with a special star.

2. **What Is Normal?** Emphasize to students that 98.6 degrees is typically a normal body temperature (although it may differ slightly for some students). If possible, mark the thermometer to show where 98.6 degrees falls so that students will only have to indicate whether their temperature falls below or is over that standard mark.

3. **Alternatives to Thermometer.** Some schools or homes use a forehead strip to give a temperature reading. In some cases this may be a more practical means to determine whether or not a student has a fever. Investigate!

TAKING YOUR TEMPERATURE

Follow the steps listed below to take your temperature. You will need a thermometer. Put a checkmark by each step after you have completed it.

Step 1. Make sure the thermometer does not show a red line above 70 degrees. Shake it until the red line is at the bottom.

Step 2. Put the bulb end of the thermometer under your tongue. Hold it there with your mouth shut, but do not use your teeth!

Step 3. Wait about 3 minutes. Don't take it out of your mouth to keep checking the line.

Step 4. Now look at the thermometer. See where the red line comes to an end.

Step 5. Write down your temperature here:

_____

Is it 98.6? _____

Higher? _____

What is the temperature on these thermometers?

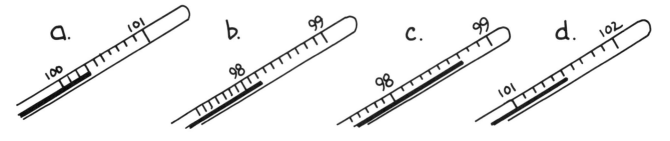

184

GETTING EXERCISE

Objective:

The student will indicate at least three ways to exercise that are personally interesting and possible for him or her.

Discussion:

Teacher: Who knows what a "couch potato" is? (someone who sits, does nothing) What do you think you would look like if you never got any exercise? ("like my dad," fat, flabby, tired) Why is it important to exercise? (get muscles, keep in shape) There are lots of ways to get exercise—and many of them are a lot of fun.

Worksheet II-77 These students want to get some exercise. Help them come up with an idea that will fit in with what they are interested in. There may be more than one good idea for each!

Answers: (suggestions)

1. Walk the dogs, run the dogs
2. Bike riding
3. Jump rope
4. Hike
5. Swim
6. Ride horseback

Extension Activities:

1. **Class Aerobics.** Borrow an exercise video for kids and have the entire class work on daily aerobics. Combined with music and laughter, this experience may turn out to be one that the entire class will look forward to.
2. **Exercise Quilt.** Have each student work on one square (paper, flannel, etc.) depicting a favorite exercise. Combine all squares to represent a "quilt" with lots of ideas for getting involved in exercise.

GETTING EXERCISE

These students want to begin an exercise program. Each is thinking about how to have fun while exercising. Help each student come up with an idea and write your suggestion on the line.

WHAT ABOUT DRUGS?

Objective:

The student will state appropriate usages of medication or drugs.

Discussion:

Teacher: Have you ever had to take any medication? What? When? (allergy pills, aspirin, et cetera) What's the difference between taking drugs that are written for you on a prescription and drugs that you can buy over the counter? (doctor must order the prescription drugs) Have you ever heard people say that drugs are bad for you or "don't do drugs"? Why? What do they mean? (some will hurt your body, can overdose easily) In general, if you take drugs that are prescribed for you and you follow the directions, you are taking drugs appropriately. You should *never* take any drugs that you can't identify or take drugs from someone you don't know. You should *never* take harmful drugs such as cocaine or acid. Only take drugs that are safe for you, ordered by a doctor, and only for as long as you need them to help you become or stay healthy.

Worksheet II-78 Sometimes it's hard to know when drugs are all right and when to stay away from them. Read these situations and write *yes* or *no* to show if you think this situation is all right or not.

Answers:

1. Yes	5. No
2. No	6. Yes
3. Yes	7. No
4. No	8. No

Extension Activities

1. **Instead of Drugs . . .** Emphasize to students that some people give the message that drugs will make them feel better or feel happy or make them feel good about themselves. Tell them that there are positive alternatives to "doing drugs" for that purpose. Have students list ways that they can feel good about themselves by doing positive things (playing basketball, painting a picture, singing with friends, etc.). Make posters to show their ideas.

2. **Good Drugs/Bad Drugs.** Students may be confused into thinking that all drugs are bad. Help inform students that many drugs (and vaccinations) have cured terrible diseases and keep people alive. Follow medicine reports in magazines and newspapers and have interested students follow up on researching some drug breakthroughs that have helped civilization (e.g. polio vaccinations, measles, mumps shots, etc.).

WHAT ABOUT DRUGS?

Here are some situations involving drug use. Write *yes* if you think this is a good or appropriate use of drugs. Write *no* if you think it is not.

1. I have a headache...
I will take an aspirin.

_____

2. Here, take these pills. They will make you feel great!

_____

3. The doctor gave me a prescription to take this medicine.

_____

4. The doctor wrote a prescription for this medicine for my brother, but I'll take it.

_____

5. My dad left some alcohol in his glass. I'll finish it for him.

_____

6. Ooooh...I feel so terrible. I'll have some of this medicine that my mother said I should take

_____

7. My friend gave me some drugs to take. I know my friend really cares about me. He wouldn't give me anything that would hurt me.

_____

8. I heard that if I take a lot of these diet pills, I'll feel real good. I think I'll try it even though I'm not on a diet.

_____

NUTRITION

Objective:

The student will identify a well-balanced meal consisting of items from the four basic food groups (milk, protein, fruits/vegetables, bread).

Discussion:

Teacher: Have you heard people talk about "junk" food? What do they mean by that term? (not very nutritious, but usually tastes pretty good!) Most of us really enjoy eating food that sometimes may not be the best for us. It's important to keep what you eat in balance or eat enough of the right kinds of foods to keep you healthy. As long as you are eating well, your body can handle some of the sweets and "junk" food that you love without making that your total meal. What kinds of food are good to eat, good for your body? (fruits, vegetables, milk, etc.) Usually people group food into four areas— milk, protein, fruits/vegetables, and bread. You should eat something from those four areas every day to keep you body healthy and at its best.

Worksheet II-79 This worksheet shows five meals that a student is going to eat for lunch. Keep in mind the four main food groups and decide whether or not you think it is a nutritious meal. Write *yes* or *no* on the line to show your answer. Then we'll discuss what you think.

Answers: (may vary)

1. Yes (all four groups represented)
2. No
3. No
4. Yes
5. Yes

Extension Activities:

1. **You Are What You Eat.** Have students list what they ate for breakfast (or improvise!) and use construction paper, markers, and so on to form the shape of a person using those food items. (For example, two bacon strip legs, cereal box head, scrambled egg hair, etc.)

2. **Food Groups.** Students may be unfamiliar with which food items are considered part of which of the main food groups. Each day (for several days) you may highlight one of the groups and have students collect pictures, empty cartons, or drawings of foods which would be considered part of that group.

NUTRITION

Take a look at what these students are eating for lunch. Write *yes* if you think it is a nutritious meal; write *no* if you think it is not.

Meal 1 _____

      glass of milk
      hamburger on bun
      french fries
      apple

Meal 2 _____

      candy bar
      potato chips
      can of soda

Meal 3 _____

      glass of milk
      carrot sticks

Meal 4 _____

      glass of ice water
      tuna casserole
      banana
      bread and butter

Meal 5 _____

      glass of milk
      cheese and sausage pizza
      green beans
      ice cream

AVOIDING UNHEALTHY HABITS

Objective:

Given an example of an unhealthy habit, the student will provide an example of a healthy alternative behavior.

Discussion:

Teacher: Does anyone know what a habit is? (something you do without thinking) A *habit* is something that you do, usually without even thinking about it, because you get used to doing it over and over. What's the first thing you do when you get home from school? (eat, change clothes, do homework) Do any of you find yourself doing something while your brain is still asleep and then you suddenly realize that you just did it out of habit? Any examples? As long as your habit is a good one, it's no problem. But sometimes you find yourself involved in bad or unhealthy habits which can be hard to break. Today we're going to think about breaking bad habits by substituting good ones.

Worksheet II-80 These students have been doing some things that they wish they could change. Help them change their bad habit into something positive. Draw or write about something that each student could do instead.

Answers: (suggestions)

1. Read in bed/turn off the light
2. Start bicycling every day/chew gum
3. Organize books the night before/start getting up earlier
4. Order a smaller pizza/don't eat at pizza places
5. Put a bar of soap next to the sink by the door/wash hands every time you enter the house

Extension Activities:

1. **Minor Behavior Modification.** Have students learn to become aware of their behavior by recording one simple behavior each day for several days. Choose a behavior that is relatively frequent (e.g., number of times you brush teeth, wash hands, take the dog out). Were they surprised to find out how many times they engaged in the behavior without consciously being aware of it? Then train them to pair another behavior with the first behavior, such as cleaning out the sink every time they brush their teeth or check

the mailbox when they take the dog out, and so on. Is it easier to do the second behavior if you link it to the first?

2. **Smoking Survey.** Smoking is generally accepted as an unhealthy habit. Have students conduct a survey in which they poll classmates and adults to find out whether or not smokers wish they could quit, have tried to quit, have quit, or do not wish to change this behavior. Is smoking popular among students? Do students think more adults smoke or don't smoke? There are lots of informational questions that could be raised. (If smoking is an inappropriate topic, chose another habit or issue. Survey students to find out what they perceive is their worst habit, etc.)

II–80

AVOIDING UNHEALTHY HABITS

These students have gotten into some unhealthy habits. Can you help them think of at least one way to break or change the habit by doing something that is healthy or different? Draw your picture or write your answer next to each situation.

Instead of: Try:

1. It's midnight, I know I have to get up really early tomorrow for school, but I'm used to watching TV every night.

2. I know smoking is bad, but I can't seem to quit.

3. The bus is here already? Where are my books? Where is my coat? I can't find my homework!

4. I really want to lose some weight, but whenever I see a pizza I have to eat the whole thing!

5. I keep forgetting to wash my hands after I've been outside!

DANGEROUS SITUATIONS

Objective:

The student will recognize potentially dangerous situations and state possible unhealthy outcomes.

Discussion:

Teacher: Has anyone seen my black rattlesnake? I lost him somewhere in this room. Oh, I'm just kidding. But what if I really did lose a poisonous snake in this room? What could happen? (could have bitten someone) Part of leading a healthy life is being careful with dangerous things. Can you help me list some things that you think are pretty dangerous? (bombs, guns, etc.) What do you think is the best thing to do if you find yourself in a dangerous situation? (leave, ask for help, find an adult)

    Worksheet II-81 Here are some students who are in some situations that could end up as pretty dangerous. Tell why each is dangerous and what the student in each situation should do. Draw or write your answers on the side.

Answers: (suggestions)

1. Dog could bite/student should leave area, call for help
2. Stranger/leave immediately, tell an adult
3. Could start a fire/leave them alone, throw them away
4. Troublemakers, could involve student/say no/have something else to do
5. Could be loaded/don't touch it, tell an adult

Extension Activities:

1. **Role-playing.** Have students act out the potentially dangerous situations, coming up with alternative endings. Have them practice saying no in many different ways!

2. **Super Student.** Create a "Super Student" superhero who comes to the rescue when students find themselves in dangerous situations. Students may wish to design a costume and draw a life-size figure. When discussion situations, refer to the figure and ask, "What would Super Student do?"

DANGEROUS SITUATIONS

These students are in some situations which could be dangerous. For each situation, list one reason why this is a dangerous or what might happen. Then draw or explain what the student should do next.

SITUATION: WHY?   HE/SHE SHOULD:

1. I don't know that dog! He sure has big teeth!

2. Come here. I want to give you something. / Who is he?

3. I wonder if these matches are still good.

4. Hey, come on with us. We're going to have some fun in the park scaring people.

5. Is that a real gun?

FOLLOWING SAFETY RULES

Objective:

The student will explain and comply with rules that are intended to ensure safety.

Discussion:

Teacher: How many of you have ever ridden on a roller coaster? Do they have a rule about keeping your hands inside and not standing up? Why? (safety) What might happen if you broke the rule? (accident) There are some rules that you should follow just because they are good ways to make sure you stay safe. Can anyone think of any safety rules around school? (no talking during fire drill, no knives)

Worksheet II-82 It seems like there are rules all the time telling you what you should and should not do. Here are some examples of rules you may have heard at home or at school. Some of them are silly rules. If the rule is a good safety rule, draw a smile on the face at the end of the rule. If it is silly, draw an X on it.

Answers:

1.	Smile	6.	Smile
2.	Smile	7.	Smile
3.	X	8.	X
4.	Smile	9.	Smile
5.	X	10.	X

Extension Activities:

1. **Old Rules.** Teachers' magazines often reprint rules for teaching and keeping the school from the turn of the century which now seem extremely humorous. Obtain such a list, or locate laws that are sometimes still on the books for some states that seem silly now. (Don't park your horse on the courthouse square after noon, etc.) Discuss why the old rules were important even though they seem silly now. Will our rules seem outrageous in 100 years?

2. **Safety Is Not Silly.** Have students compile a list of school rules. While some (gum-chewing, quiet at lunch) may seem unfair or unnecessary, have students think about why they promote safety. Would an alien, visiting from another planet, think the school rules were silly? How would you explain to him/her/it why the rule was necessary?

FOLLOWING SAFETY RULES

Some of these rules are safety rules; others are silly rules. If it is a safety rule, draw a smile on the face. If it is a silly rule, put an X on the face.

1. Wear your seat belt in the car.

2. Don't tell anyone where the key to your house is kept.

3. Don't brush your teeth while standing on your head.

4. Come home before it gets dark outside.

5. Only hitchhike with young drivers.

6. Don't talk during a fire drill.

7. Lock your bike when you leave it outside.

8. Don't put paper clips in your hair.

9. When strangers call on the phone, don't tell them if you are home alone.

10. Call the police if you oversleep and need a ride to school.

Dear Parents,

Many families are two-worker families these days, which sometimes leaves children coming home to an empty house. Latchkey living is part of life. The lessons we will be working on are directed primarily to children who need to learn safe, resourceful behaviors without parents directly in charge, but also to any student, latchkey or not, because all students can benefit from knowing how to handle those situations in which there is no one specifically watching them. The key is teaching responsible, safe behaviors.

If your child comes home to a locked house, be sure to go over your plans for him or her. What should your child do if he or she has a problem, question, homework, visitor, phone call, or tummy ache? Be sure to have emergency procedures lined up, and *always* have a person designated as his "support" person—a backup adult.

Open communication of expectations between adults and children is a requirement in situations like these. You want to trust your child, and he or she needs to have your approval.

Sincerely,

_____

Teacher

Skill Sheet #12: Progress Report

+ mastered
√ emerging
− not mastered

Student name	Key	Knowing rules	Time—wisely	Backup plan	Comments

KEEPING THE KEY

Objective:

If appropriate, the student will designate a safe place to keep his or her housekey and use the place habitually.

Discussion:

Teacher: How do you think I got into the school this morning? (through door) When the door is locked, how could I get in? (key) How many of you have a key to get into your house or know where the key is? Sometimes you hear the term *latchkey* or latchkey children. That refers to having a key that will open a door, usually the front door, to a house. Why would children have a key to their house? (let them in when parents aren't home) Can you think of some good places to keep a very important key? (around neck, on chain, etc.)

Worksheet II-83 Here are some examples of students who need to know where their housekey is. Circle the students who are keeping their key in a safe place. Put an X on those who are not. Then we will discuss your reasons.

Answers:

1. O		5. X
2. X		6. O
3. X		7. O
4. O		8. X

Extension Activities:

1. **Key Hunt.** Have a collection of old keys for use with this activity. Have students hide the keys around the room, marking "their" key with tape, initials, and so on. Students take turns searching for hidden keys. When all keys are found, discuss which places were good hiding places, which were too inconvenient to keep a key in, and possibly which locations may have been forgotten. Stress the importance of knowing where the key is as well as finding a "good" place.

2. **Key Stories.** Have students write stories in which they "turn into" their housekey for a day. Ask them to write of their experiences of being lost, being carried away by a bird, opening the house of a famous person, and so on.

KEEPING THE KEY

Some of these students are keeping their key in a safe place. Others are not. Circle the students who are keeping their key safely. Put an X on the others.

KNOWING THE RULES

Objective:

The student will state appropriate rules for activities until his or her parents return home.

Discussion:

Teacher: We've been talking about getting into the house when you get home from school. But what happens then? I'll bet you have some rules to follow until your parents get home. Who has some examples? (do homework, stay off the phone, etc.) Why do you think your parents have rules like that? (make sure you're safe and do something useful)

Worksheet II-84 Many families have rules that students are supposed to follow when they get home from school, especially if your parents aren't there. Here are some examples. Circle the ones that are used in your house. You can add some at the bottom.

Extension Activities:

1. **Latchkey Life.** Families are very diverse in their expectations of students after school. If you have students who say they have no rules or supervision (which is possible), change the focus of the discussion to safety; that is, what do *you* do to make sure you are safe until your parents get home? Use this as a discussion topic to consider how diverse people and families are. One family is not better because they are or are not all home at the same time. People are different and yet function effectively in many ways. Much responsibility is often given to young children. As a teacher, strive to praise the acceptance of that responsibility and promote the idea of "helping out the family."

2. **Keys to the Future.** Have each student cut out a large cardboard or paper key (you may want to cut a stencil first) and add his name and future dream or occupation. Talk about how a key opens up something. What will be opened up to them in the future? A good job? Lots of money? A big house? Let them dream!

Name _____   Date _____

II–84

KNOWING THE RULES

Here are some rules that you may have been given to follow when you get home from school. Circle the ones that are used in your house. You may wish to add some that are not on the list.

Take off your shoes before you walk on the carpet.

Take the dog out right away.

Start your homework.

If you make a snack, put the dishes in the sink when you're done.

Don't tie up the phone by talking too long.

Look on the refrigerator for messages.

Clean your room.

Call mom/dad as soon as you get in.

Don't have friends over.

Babysit your little brother/sister.

_____

_____

_____

_____

_____

_____

_____

_____

_____

USING TIME WISELY

Objective:

The student will identify ways to use unsupervised time at home in a wise or helpful manner.

Discussion:

Teacher: What would happen if you didn't have parents telling you what to do with your time? ("It'd be fun.") If you knew you still had to go to school the next day, do you think you would get all your work done? Even if no one was telling you to do it? (some yes, some no) How many of you could supervise yourself?

Worksheet II-85 Read the cartoon story about two boys, Tom and Kirk, and what they did one afternoon after school. When you're done, let's list all the things they got done before their mother got home from work.

Answers: (suggestions)

Had a snack
Cleaned the kitchen
Rode bikes
Cooked supper
Set the table
Practiced spelling

Extension Activities:

1. **Surprise Night.** Have students take a cue from Tom and Kirk and plan a pleasant surprise for their parent(s) one afternoon after school. It would not have to be something as elaborate as dinner, but have students commit to one small thing that they will do to help out or pleasantly surprise a working parent. Ideas: flowers in a vase, homework done without being asked, pleasant greeting at the door, and so on. The following morning, discuss what resulted. (Or have students draw their parent's face!)

2. **Checklist.** Have students write up a list of activities that they should complete after school. With parent cooperation, have students complete the activities, check each off, and have the checklist signed and commented on by the parent. Students may find that a written list helps them achieve a sense of accomplishment, and parents may also benefit from the organization and time taken to recognize what their child has done in their absence.

USING TIME WISELY

Read the story below about Tom and his brother Kirk. Think about ways that they used their time.

HAVING A BACKUP PLAN

Objective:

The student will state a backup plan for anticipating problems related to entering and staying in the house until his or her parents arrive.

Discussion:

Teacher: What would you do if you arrived at home and realized that your key was missing? (call a neighbor, call parents) What would you do if your mom told you to take the dog out, but the dog was limping and seemed to be in pain? (call parents, take to vet) Sometimes plans don't go the way you think they should, and then you have to come up with a backup plan. It's easier to think of a good backup plan *before* problems happen instead of in the middle of a problem. Today I want you to think about making plans for when things go wrong and you are home by yourself or without your parents.

Worksheet II-86 Here are some examples of things that could go wrong or situations that you need to know what your parents would want you to do if they would occur. Write down what you think you could do in each situation.

Answers: (suggestions)

1. Call a neighbor, try again, check to make sure it's the right key
2. Tell them to go next door
3. Tell them to come back later, take a message
4. Help him over the phone, set up a later time
5. Don't go in, call your parents
6. Call a neighbor or parents, carefully check out the source, call fire department
7. Call your parents and let them know, have the caller call parents at work
8. Know where the flashlight is, turn off switches, oven, and so on

Extension Activities:

1. **Emergency Box.** Compile a checklist of items that could be helpful in a "tight" situation and have students gather them into an "emergency box." Items could include flashlight and batteries, emergency numbers or procedures written down, an extra key for the main door (or alternative entry), wrapped food items (granola bar, potato chips), Band-aids or first aid equipment, paper and pen, and so on. Communicate with parents to explain the activity and enlist their cooperation. Where will the items be kept? Who should use them?

2. **Backup People.** Most students will have identified a neighbor or relative to be "on call" in an emergency or problem situation, such as being locked out or frightened at home. Have students identify the person and go over procedures for how that person will be contacted in the event of such a situation. Home drills should be conducted with parent awareness and support.

II–86

HAVING A BACKUP PLAN

Here are some situations that could arise if you were home alone or waiting for your parents. Think about what you could do in each situation. Write your answer on the line.

1. The key won't open the door. The door seems to be sticking.

_____

_____

2. You are home alone and someone you don't know comes to the door and says he wants to use your telephone.

_____

_____

3. You are home alone and someone you don't know comes to the door and says he is supposed to pick something up.

_____

_____

4. Your friend calls and wants to come over to get some help with his homework, but your parents don't like your friends to come over when they're not home.

_____

_____

5. You arrive home and find that the door is unlocked and open a little bit.

_____

_____

6. You smell smoke coming from the garage.

_____

_____

7. You get a telephone call that is very important, and you need to let your parents know right away.

_____

_____

8. The electricity goes out.

_____

_____

part III

Community Independence

PARENT LETTER #13   COMMUNITY PLACES AND PEOPLE

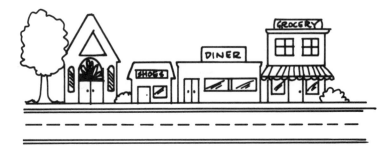

Dear Parents,

We are beginning a series of lessons on developing independence in our community. I'm sure you will agree that eventually our students need to acquire the ability to use community resources and get around in the community to help them get the things they want and need.

Our first focus is on identifying places in the community and people who work there. We will be talking about locating local restaurants, shopping malls, parks, churches, temples, leisure events, and the library. If possible, we will try to visit these places and find out what is offered at each.

You can help by taking your child to as many public places as possible and exposing him or her to the wide variety of things to do and learn in our own community.

Thanks!

Sincerely,

_____
Teacher

Skill Sheet #13: Progress Report

+ mastered
√ emerging
− not mastered

Student name	Restaurant	Shopping mall	Park	Churches	Movie theater	Sporting events	Arcade	Video store	Public library	Museum	Comments

RESTAURANTS

Objective:

The student will be able to state the names, general locations of, and general services of several restaurants in the area.

Discussion:

Teacher: I'm going to describe a place where I had dinner last night, and you try to tell me where I was. (describe the facilities, menu, etc., of a local restaurant) Where was I? (restaurant) What exactly is a restaurant? (place where someone else cooks for the general public) A *restaurant* is a public eating place. Who can help me name three of them? What is the same or similar about each? What is different? (cost, service, menu items, location) Who are some people or workers you would find at a restaurant? (waiter, hostess, etc.)

Worksheet III-87 This worksheet describes five restaurants that might be in a community. Then it describes five students who could get what they are looking for at the different restaurants. Match each student with an appropriate restaurant for him or her to eat at.

Answers:

1. c
2. d
3. e
4. b
5. a

Extension Activities:

1. **Restaurant Survey.** If possible, collect menus from several restaurants in your community. What is characteristic about each? Can the restaurants be grouped in several ways? (appeal to young, appeal to adults/expensive, inexpensive/extensive menu, one main item)

2. **Community Map.** Begin working on developing a community map, featuring items of interest in your community. Which restaurants would a visitor to your area be interested in? Draw a picture of the restaurant (or cut part of the menu and insert it in a drawing) and place it on the community map. Add to the map as the different community points are discussed in later lessons. Remember to plan this from a student's point of view—the most important restaurant in town may be the hamburger joint!

Name _____ Date _____

III–87

RESTAURANTS

The numbered column describes several restaurants. Match the student on the right with a restaurant that he or she may want to visit. Write the letter of the student on the line next to the restaurant.

1. MEXICAN PETE'S PLACE _____
This is a fast-food restaurant that serves tacos, beans, and other Mexican-style foods.

2. THE GARDEN SPOT _____
This is a sit-down restaurant with full-course meals, waiters, live music, and a very expensive menu.

3. MILLIE'S _____
This is a diner where you sit at a counter and order simple home-cooked meals, such as hamburgers, soup, and perhaps apple pie and ice cream for dessert.

4. BURGERS-TO-GO _____
This is a fast-food hamburger place (with fries and cookies) that is not too expensive.

a. Mike and his family want to go to a nice place with some friends, but don't want to spend a lot of money. They want to sit, talk, and not have to dress up.

b. Sherry and her friends want to go out after the school volleyball game for something to eat, but mostly they want to talk and laugh.

c. Frank wants something quick to eat, but he doesn't have a lot of time and doesn't like hamburgers.

d. Allen and his parents are celebrating his sister's graduation from college. They want to go to a very nice place. Price is no problem.

e. Debbie and Darlene want a full meal, but don't want fast food or a big bill (but they have to eat dessert!).

_____

5. CAROLYN'S COOKIN' _____
This is a sit-down restaurant that serves entire meals, has menus and waitresses or waiters, and lets you wear casual clothes, such as jeans.

III-A COMMUNITY PLACES AND PEOPLE   *LESSON 88*

SHOPPING MALL

Objective:

The student will be able to state several stores which would be likely to be found at a mall or at the local mall.

Discussion:

Teacher: Let's say I wanted to get several things on my shopping day. I want to get some new shoes, a dress, a book for a birthday present for someone, a puppy for my niece, and some tennis balls. How many stores would I have to go to? (lots) Can you think of a place that has lots of stores close together? A *mall*, or shopping mall, is a place where there is a row of stores. Why do you think that's a good idea? (easy to get to, just park once, might be enclosed and warm) Who are some people or workers you would find at a shopping mall? (clerk, store owners, cashier)

Worksheet III-88 Here is an example of the stores in a mall. Sharon, who is shopping, wants to get several things at the mall, but she doesn't need to go to every store. Help her plan how she could get everything she needs by putting a number on each store that she should go to.

Answers:

1. Pat's Pet Store
2. Toys
3. Photos
4. Polly's Plants
5. Beauty Boutique

Extension Activities:

1. **Our Own Mall.** If possible, have students visit a local shopping mall and take a quick inventory of the different stores that are included. If they were the mayor for a day what stores would they put in their mall? (encourage creativity) What's important? What's needed? What's wanted?

2. **Giant Mall.** Following the theme of the worksheet, have students select mall stores that they would like to have or visit at a mall and then draw, find pictures, or otherwise create impressions of what would be likely to be found in the store. Maybe students would like to pair up to be jewelry shop proprietors, pet store owners, music or video owners, skateboard repair operators, or sell exotic pets.

SHOPPING MALL

Here is a map of a shopping mall called Parkway Plaza. Look at it carefully so you are familiar with the stores and how to get to them. Then help Sharon the Shopper plan how she would go to get everything on her list. Number the stores she would visit 1, 2, 3, and so on.

Sharon's List:
    Doll
    Plant for mother
    Drop off film
    Get puppy food
    Hair spray

THE PARK

Objective:

The student will identify several activities that can take place at a public park.

Discussion:

Teacher: What's the name of a park in town? What are some things that people do there? (play basketball, swing, walk on trails, etc.) Why do you think communities have parks? (provide public with clean, safe area to relax, etc.) Most parks have some rules that go with the privilege of being able to use the park. Can you think of any? (don't litter, keep your dog on a leash, etc.) What people or workers would be at a park? (park ranger, lifeguard, etc.)

Worksheet III-89 Here is a list of some things that could happen at a park. Write *yes* if you think it should be done at a park; write *no* if you think it should not be done at a park.

Answers:

1. Yes	7. Yes
2. Yes	8. No
3. Yes	9. Yes
4. No	10. Yes
5. No	11. No
6. Yes	12. Yes

Extension Activities:

1. **Nature Walk.** Public parks sometimes offer guided tours for classes to point out interesting nature facts and teach students about ecology in action in your community. If not, plan to take your class on a walk, noting the various activities that are offered at the park.

2. **Park Rules.** Find out what specific rules are in effect at your local park department. Discuss with your students why littering is harmful or why there is no swimming without a lifeguard, and so on. Also investigate what opportunities are available through the parks and recreation department, such as softball leagues, day-camping experiences, swimming lessons, and so on.

III–89

THE PARK

Here is a list of some activities. If you think it could be done at a public park, write *yes* on the line. If you think it could not (or should not) be done at a public park, write *no*.

1. Swimming in a pool _____

2. Having a picnic _____

3. Walking on trails _____

4. Leaving pop cans and bottles _____

5. Shooting squirrels _____

6. Having a birthday party _____

7. Riding your bike _____

8. Driving a car on the baseball diamond _____

9. Swinging or using a slide _____

10. Playing frisbee with a friend _____

11. Letting your dog run loose for a long time without watching him _____

12. Playing tennis _____

III-A COMMUNITY PLACES AND PEOPLE   *LESSON 90*

HOUSES OF WORSHIP

Objective:

The student will identify and locate several houses of worship in his or her community.

Discussion:

Teacher: I'm thinking of a community place that people might go to on a weekend day. Can anyone guess? (church) Many people go to church on Sunday, but some religions have their church services on Saturday. Does anyone want to tell us about the house of worship that they go to? Can you tell us where it is located? Besides listening to a sermon, what other activities happen at your church? (youth group meeting, prayer meetings, softball practice, etc.) In our country, we have the freedom to go to whatever church we want to go, and worship the way we want to. This is a very important freedom that doesn't happen in every country. Let's think about the different houses of worship in our community and where they are. Can you help me with the names of the religious leaders? (minister, pastor, priest, rabbi, choir director, etc.)

Worksheet III-90 There are many kinds of buildings of worship, but this worksheet will show just a few of them. Match the number of each church with the student at the top who attends that place of worship. Write the number on the line.

Answers:

> Amy—2
> Adam—4
> Carolyn—1
> David—3

Extension Activities:

1. **Holidays.** Many holidays are religious (originally) in nature. Investigate the roots of these holidays and discuss the impact that each has on everyday life today. Why doesn't everyone celebrate Christmas? What is Hanukkah? In the midst of December festivities, you may want to have a person of the Jewish faith visit your class and explain the significance of this event.

2. **Historical Churches.** Many churches have an interesting history. Check out the church buildings in your area. When was each founded? Dig up some local historical trivia!

HOUSES OF WORSHIP

Here is a map of part of a small town. The houses of worship are marked with a star (*). Match the students below with the church or synagogue that they attend. Use the clues next to each student to help you match them up. Write the number of the church or synagogue next to the student who goes there.

Amy goes to a large church surrounded by many trees. She attends church early in the morning on Sunday. It is called mass. She is a member of a Catholic church. _____

Adam worships on Saturday at a building called a synagogue. Adam is Jewish. _____

Carolyn goes to a church on Sunday morning. She attends a Protestant church with a white fence around it. _____

David is also going to a Protestant church, but his is a different kind. His church has bricks on the front. _____

III-A COMMUNITY PLACES AND PEOPLE *LESSON 91*

MOVIE THEATER

Objective:

The student will be able to state the location of the theater and procedure for attending a movie there.

Discussion:

Teacher: Who here has seen a good movie lately? What did you see? If you wanted to see a movie, but didn't want to rent a video, where could you go? (local theater) Let's say I was new in town and I didn't know anything about getting to the movie or how to get a ticket or popcorn or anything! Could you help me? What people would you find working at a movie theater? (usher, ticket-taker, counter clerk, etc.)

Worksheet III-91 Here is a scene from a typical movie theater. What are some things that you see? (concession stand, rest rooms, etc.) I want you to look carefully at the picture and answer the questions about the situation. Write *yes* or *no* on the line next to each statement.

Answers:

1. Yes
2. No
3. Yes
4. No
5. No
6. Yes

Extension Activities:

1. **Careful Questions.** Have students write additional questions about the picture requiring careful looking and thinking. Exchange the questions and discuss the clues. Were some more obvious than others?
2. **Ratings.** Use a local movie guide from the newspaper and discuss which movies the students have seen. What do the ratings G, PG, PG-13, and R indicate? Have students give movie reviews of pictures that they particularly enjoyed. Do they have to be violent to be enjoyed? Have students develop their own rating system, for example, funny, good characters, good story, exciting, and so on.

MOVIE THEATER

These people want to see the movie *Mutant Frogs That Ate New York*. Look carefully at the picture and answer *yes* or *no* to the questions about the moviegoers and the theater.

1. The frog movie is just about to start. _____
2. It will cost the boy $4.50 to get a ticket. _____
3. There are two movies playing at this theater. _____
4. The ticket-taker is a woman. _____
5. You can get hamburgers at the snack stand. _____
6. The frog movie is in Theater 2. _____

III-A COMMUNITY PLACES AND PEOPLE   *LESSON 92*

SPORTING EVENTS

Objective:

The student will be able to determine location, times, prices, and other pertinent information about selected sporting events in the community.

Discussion:

Teacher: Who here has ever been to a basketball game? Where? Has anyone ever watched a football game at the high school? Why do you think so many people are interested in sports and sporting events? (fun, social, like to watch winners) What sporting events are available in our community, either to participate in or to watch? What people or workers are connected with sporting events? (coaches, players, ushers, broadcasters, et cetera) What is a *spectator*? (someone who watches) A spectator is a person who comes to a game to watch rather than to play. What games do you like to be a spectator at?

Worksheet III-92 Here is an article that you might see in a newspaper, telling about a sporting event that you might want to attend. Read the article carefully and see if you can find the answers to the questions about the game at the bottom. Write your answers on the lines.

Answers:

1. Lakeside Lasers, Northside Rangers   5. $1.50
2. Basketball   6. 7:30 P.M.
3. Lakeside gymnasium   7. 50 cents
4. 6:30 P.M.   8. Yes

Extension Activities:

1. **Sports Reading.** Have students bring in newspaper articles about their favorite teams. After reading the article, have them write comprehension questions about the article. Exchange questions among students.

2. **Sports Math.** Following the same ideas as sports reading, have students use sports statistics from games or player records to write math problems or story problems. Exchange problems among students.

© 1992 by The Center for Applied Research in Education

Name _____   Date _____

III–92

SPORTING EVENTS

Here is an article telling about a basketball game in a community. Read it carefully; then try to answer the questions on the lines below.

The Lakeside Lasers are going to play Northside High School Rangers in a championship basketball game on Friday, October 26, at 7:30 P.M. This will be a home game for the Lasers in the Lakeside High School gymnasium. Doors will open at 6:30 P.M. with tickets going on sale at both the front and side doors of the gym. Tickets are $2.50 for adults, $1.50 for students, and $1.00 for children under 12. Refreshments will be available at the concession stand throughout the game. Programs listing the players will be sold for 50 cents.

1. Which two teams are going to play? _____

2. What sport are they playing? _____

3. Where will the game be played? _____

4. What time can a person get into the gym to watch? _____

5. How much will it cost for a student to attend? _____

6. What time does the game start? _____

7. How much are the programs? _____

8. Will people be able to get something to drink there? _____

THE ARCADE

Objective:

The student will be able to identify procedures for operating machines in a public arcade.

Discussion:

Teacher: Who knows what a pinball machine is? Who can tell me the name of a good video game? Which ones are the most fun? Where do you go to play those games? (mall, stores, arcade) What do you need to play? (money or tokens) A video arcade or games arcade is a store that has a selection of machines that you can play with for fun. Where is an arcade nearby?

Worksheet III-93 This worksheet shows two types of machines that you might find at an arcade. One is a pinball machine, and the other is a video game (maze). Look at the pictures and see if you can fill in the missing words on the lines below.

Answers:

PINBALL— 1. token   VIDEO GAME—1. token
              2. starter   2. token
              3. ball   3. button
              4. points   4. joystick
              5. flipper controls   5. up
              6. five   6. right
              7. two   7. points

Extension Activities:

1. **My Favorite Game.** Have students draw their favorite pinball or video game, including monsters, people, controls, and so on. Encourage them to label all parts. Then have students write out directions for how to operate the machine and how to use strategies (if known) to win the game. Encourage lots of colors and pizzazz!

2. **Video Contest.** If a video game is available on a school computer, arrange for your class to spend some time, allowing each student time to practice and play a video game. Then have a class tournament, either with teams or partners or individual students trying to beat their "personal best."

THE ARCADE

These students are at an arcade with lots of machines available to play for fun. At this arcade, all of the machines operate on tokens. Each token costs 25 cents, or one quarter. Read the directions for operating each machine; then complete the statements below.

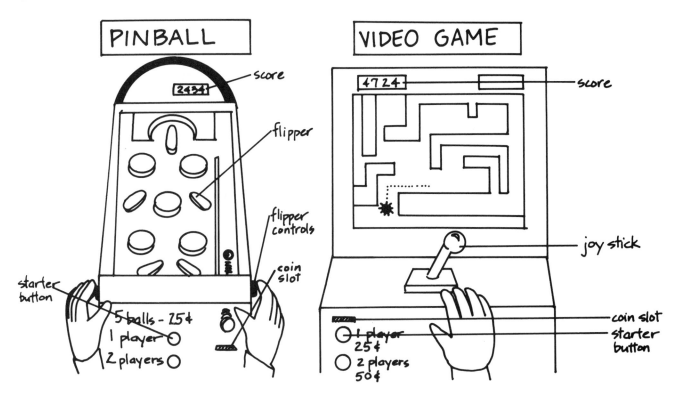

PINBALL GAME

1. First you have to put a _____ into the coin slot.
2. You have to push the _____ button to begin the game.
3. Pull the spring on the side of the machine, and the _____ will shoot up and play will begin.
4. When the ball hits the targets, you will get _____.
5. Move the _____ _____ to try to keep the ball in play.
6. On this game, you have _____ balls to use in one game.
7. On this game, up to _____ players can play one game.

VIDEO GAME

1. This machine won't take quarters, so you will have to take a quarter to the person in charge and get a _____.
2. Put the _____ into the coin or token slot.
3. Press the starter _____ to start the game.
4. The stick that moves your player around is called the _____.
5. If you move the stick up, your player will go _____.
6. If you move your stick to the right, your player will go to the _____.
7. If your player kills the monsters or enemies, you will get _____ on the scoreboard.

THE VIDEO STORE

Objective:

The student will be able to state the location of and general services of a video store.

Discussion:

Teacher: Does anyone know what the letters "VCR" stand for? (video cassette recorder) What do we mean when we talk about a "video"? A *videotape* is a recording of something you can show on a television screen. But words that you use a lot sometimes get shortened. When we talk about videotapes, we usually call them—what? (videos) What's the place where you can go and rent or buy videos? (video store) What kinds of videos are there? Are they all movies? (cartoons, exercise tapes, instructional tapes, etc.) What workers do you think you'd find at a video store? (cashier, manager) Where could you get videos around here? (video store, supermarket, pharmacy, etc.)

Worksheet III-94 Here is a student named Victor (the Video King) who loves to get videotapes. Take a look at his list and write down the letter of the section where he would probably find each tape.

Answers:

1. G
2. F
3. C
4. B

Extension Activities:

1. **Classifying Videos.** Have students give examples of movies or tapes that would fit the various categories at a typical video store. When visiting a video store, take note of all the different types of videos that are now available.

2. **How to . . . .** Check out a "how to" video from a local store. Expose students to the educational aspect of learning how to do something from watching instructions on a tape. Perhaps students would like to make their own!

Name _____ Date _____

III–94

THE VIDEO STORE

Here is the inside of a video store. Use the information signs to figure out where Victor the Video King would probably find the videotapes he wants. Write the letter of the section on the line next to Victor's choice.

1. "Woody Woodpecker" cartoons _____

2. "How to Build Up Your Arm Muscles in 30 Days" _____

3. "The Invasion of the Little Green Men from Saturn" _____

4. "The Cowboy and the Cactus" _____

227

THE PUBLIC LIBRARY

Objective:

The student will be able to state the location of and general services provided by the local public library.

Discussion:

Teacher: Who has been to the public library recently? What's a library for? (reading and borrowing books) Aha! I thought you'd say that! But I want you to think harder! Your public library can do a lot more for you than provide you with books to borrow for free. Start thinking of other things that you or your parents might have used the library for. (copier machine, check out videos, computer searches for books or magazines, night courses for adults, summer reading clubs, phone books from other cities, newspapers, records, storytelling sessions for children, etc.) Who are some workers at a library? (librarian, researchers, audiovisual technician)

Worksheet III-95 A public library is a wonderful place to find out about a lot of things. On this worksheet, I want you to list all the things a library can do for you and the community. We will try to visit the library soon to add to your list and learn about the things you can borrow, do, and learn there.

Answers: (will vary)

Check with your local library to find out what services are offered.

Extension Activities:

1. **Library Visit.** Have your local librarian give your students a tour of the different sections of the library, classification of books, audiovisual products, tips on conducting research, and special events sponsored by the library. Conclude by making sure each student has a library card.

2. **Library Research.** Have students research how public libraries got started, how many books are in the local library, which are the most popular books, how many books are checked out each year, and so on. Have students pose questions that they are interested in and assign students in small groups or pairs to use the library to find some answers.

THE PUBLIC LIBRARY

Your public library provides more for you than letting you borrow books. Find out what else it can offer you! Can you find or think of 15 things?

1. _____

2. _____

3. _____

4. _____

5. _____

6. _____

7. _____

8. _____

9. _____

10. _____

11. _____

12. _____

13. _____

14. _____

15. _____

III-A COMMUNITY PLACES AND PEOPLE   *LESSON 96*

A MUSEUM

Objective:

The student will be able to state the location of and purpose for a museum.

Discussion:

Teacher: I was wearing a necklace the other day, and someone came up to me and said, "Wow! That looks like something out of a museum!" What did he mean by that? (old, interesting, valuable) What is a museum? (place to see things of interest and value) A *museum* is a display of rare or interesting objects or things that people would like to learn about. Can you name any museums? (may have a local museum, natural history museum, wax museum) How is a museum like a library? (open to public, special collections) How is a museum different from a library? (can't take things home, museum might have books but mostly other items) Who are some workers that you would find at a museum? (caretaker/curator, custodian, archeologist, other scientists)

Worksheet III-96 If you have never been to a museum, you might be interested to know about some of the different exhibits that might be there. This worksheet lists some exhibits that could be at a museum. Circle the ones that sound interesting to you. Perhaps you'll get to visit a museum that has an exhibit like it!

Extension Activities:

1. **Museum Ideas.** Many museums will send free information brochures or flyers publicizing special events. Check for displays of exhibits and call them to the attention of your students. If a local museum is featuring something special, arrange for a class tour.

2. **Museums A to Z.** If you can take a day for a field trip to a museum, have students make a list of the interesting things that they saw at the end of the day (A = ant farm, B = bug collection, C = Chinese jewelry, etc.).

A MUSEUM

The following exhibits might be in a museum that you could visit. Circle the ones that you think would be interesting to see and learn about.

1. Ancient mummies from Egypt

2. Airplanes that were used in World Wars I and II

3. A giant heart that you can walk through

4. A submarine that was captured from the Germans in World War II

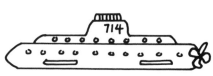

5. Chickens hatching from eggs

6. Sand paintings done by Navajo Indians

7. Dolls from around the world

8. Historic villages that show what life was like hundreds of years ago

9. A movie that shows what the Earth looks like from outer space

10. Uniforms and baseball mitts from famous baseball players

Dear Parents,

As we continue our investigation into the buildings and services of our community, we will now be stressing more practical problems. What should your child do if he or she needs a light for his or her bike? What if your child needs to have the cat taken to the vet for pills? What if you simply send your child on an errand to purchase something for you? Can your child be trusted? Does your child know where to go? What to do?

While we will be discussing the various services that people and places in the community can offer, it is very important that your child is exposed to community places and knows where he or she could go—or where you want him or her to go—for assistance. For example, is your child allowed to go to the store alone? If his or her hair is too long, does he or she know the procedure for lining up a haircut?

Gaining independence is a long process, one that we allow children to share a little bit at a time. When your child is ready, allow him or her to exert his or her independence and practice being resourceful. Watch your child—but give him or her some experiences to grow in independence!

Sincerely,

_____

Teacher

Skill Sheet #14: Progress Report

+ mastered
√ emerging
− not mastered

Student name	Shoe repair	Returning clothing	Pet/vet	Haircut	Card	Stamps	Bike tire	Comments

GETTING A SHOE REPAIRED

Objective:

Given the problem of having to have a shoe repaired, the student will identify a likely community resource and appropriate procedures to solve the problem.

Discussion:

Teacher: During the next few lessons, you will be given a typical, everyday problem that you will have to solve. It will involve something that you need to do, get, have repaired, or find, and you will have to figure out which community store or person could best help you. Our first problem is this: you need to have a heel put back on a shoe. Let's come up with a plan for working through this problem. What do we need to do? examples: find out (1) where a shoe store is, (2) cost, (3) how to get to the store, (4) when will it be finished.

Worksheet III-97 Here is a worksheet to help you work through the problem. You can use whatever resources (person, phone book, past experience) necessary to find someone or someplace to help you. When everyone is done, we'll compare answers and see what you've come up with.

Answers: (will vary)

Be sure to compare prices, services offered from different repair stores, and so on. Have students compare results. This project may take a day or two while students do the calling, asking, or legwork required to find the answers.

Extension Activities:

1. **Yellow Pages Connection.** Use your local Yellow Pages business directory to identify several shoe repair stores or places where this service is offered. Designate one student to call each store to get estimates on repairs.

2. **Shoes and More.** Have students find out what other services are available at the place where they would go to get a shoe repaired. Does the store also repair leather handbags? Does the store offer belts for sale? Can they dye shoes different colors? Most stores do not simply offer one service, and time and effort can be saved on later when the student needs to find a repair service for something else.

GETTING A SHOE REPAIRED

Problem: The heel on your shoe needs to be replaced.

Find out

1. What store you will go to.

2. How much it will cost.

3. How long it will take.

4. If you will get an identification slip or tag to claim your shoe.

5. (afterward) If you are satisfied with the work.

RETURNING CLOTHING

Objective:

Given the problem of having to return an item of clothing to the original retail store, the student will identify appropriate procedures to do so.

Discussion:

Teacher: Have you ever wanted a certain sweater for your birthday and your mother said she bought it for you but when you took it out of the box it looked like it would fit your pet cat instead? What would you do if you had to return the sweater for one that was your correct size? (find out what store it came from, find sales receipt, know your correct size) Let's come up with a plan.

Worksheet III-98 This student is having some problems returning jeans that don't fit. In each situation, figure out what the problem is and what the student needs to do. Write your answer on the lines.

Answers:

1. Have a rip/find out what store they came from
2. Wrong color or style/sales receipt
3. Don't fit/needs to know size

Extension Activities:

1. **What's My Size.** Have each student determine his or her present clothing sizes for shirt, pants, shoes, and so on. Some clothing is marked only "small," "medium," or "large." Discuss what sizes will probably fit. Have students use present clothing sizes or try on sample clothes to estimate.

2. **Sales Receipt.** Have students bring in a sales receipt from a recent purchase. Carefully go over what information is recorded on the slip. (store, date of purchase, method of payment, etc.) Discuss why it is important to save the receipt.

RETURNING CLOTHING

This student is trying to return a pair of jeans. What is the problem in each case? What should she do next time?

1.

They have a rip on the side.

I can see that... but they did not come from this store. I can't take them back.

Problem: _____ She needs: _____

2.

I like them, but they don't go with my sweater.

They are from this store, but I think they were on sale. I need to know how much they cost when they were sold.

Problem: _____ She needs: _____

3.

These don't fit either.

You've been back here four times. Why don't you find out and REMEMBER what size you are?

Problem: _____ She needs: _____

Could I try these on before I buy them?

YES! YES! YES!

TAKING A PET TO THE VET

Objective:

Given the problem of having to take a pet to the veterinarian, the student will identify a likely community vet or resource and appropriate procedures to solve the problem.

Discussion:

Teacher: How many of you have pets? What kinds do you have? When your pet needs shots or is sick, what is a community person or place that you may have to use? (veterinarian clinic or hospital) Do you know the name and location of the place where your vet works? Here is your problem for today: Let's say that you need to get your pet to the vet, first, for just ordinary reasons and, second, in an emergency. Think about how you would handle this; then do some investigating to get real answers.

Worksheet III-99 This worksheet shows two situations in which you might have to take your pet to the vet or clinic. Think about each question and write down what you would do. You might have to make some phone calls to find out real answers.

Extension Activities:

1. **Pet Services.** Have students call local animal hospitals or veterinarians and get prices on routine pet services, such as boarding, grooming, vaccinations, neutering, or baths. Make a chart comparing information. Find out any additional services that are offered.

2. **Exotic Pets.** Some pet stores sell unusual pets, such as ferrets, skunks, or monkeys. Find out why this is discouraged by veterinarians, what care is required, and who services animals such as those in a zoo or nature center. Discuss reasons why exotic animals would be difficult to care for as pets.

Name _____ Date _____

III–99

TAKING A PET TO THE VET

Here are some situations that you might have to figure out if you own a pet. Decide what you would do in each case and write your answers on the lines.

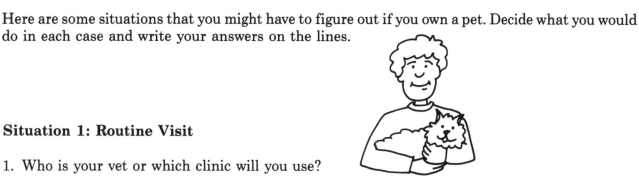

Situation 1: Routine Visit

1. Who is your vet or which clinic will you use?

2. How will you get there?

3. Do you need to make an appointment or can you just drop in?

4. Do you need to pay right away or will the vet bill you?

5. How often do you have to take your pet back? For what reason?

Situation 2: Emergency Visit

1. Who will you call for help or information?

2. How will you get your pet there?

3. Who can you call around your home to help you with your pet?

4. Do you have a cage or carrying case to put your pet in?

5. Where can you get towels or rags to wrap up your pet if you need them?

GETTING A HAIRCUT

Objective:

Given the problem of having to set up an appointment for a haircut, the student will identify a likely community resource and procedures for completing the activity.

Discussion:

Teacher: Your problem for today has to do with something that you have probably already done at some time in the last few months or even sooner! It's . . . getting your hair cut. I'm not going to give you many clues this time. Think about what you would have to do to get that great look you've been wanting!

Worksheet III-100 Use this worksheet to help you plan out where, when, and how you could get your hair cut. When everyone is finished with the activity, we'll compare your answers.

Answers: (will vary)

Extension Activities:

1. **Super Salon.** Have students compile a list of the various services offered by many beauty salons, including manicures, tanning beds, ear piercing, and facials. Some salons charge by the service and charge extra for washing and conditioning hair before the cut. Some do not provide styling or hair drying. Have students figure out the relative cost of each procedure at the different stores.

2. **Walk-ins versus Appointments.** Some stores do not require an appointment for getting a haircut; others insist on it. Have students categorize beauty salons (or barber shops) according to this feature. Do they prefer one over the other? Why?

GETTING A HAIRCUT

You need (and want) a haircut. Think about how you would do this. Write down your answers on the lines.

1. Where do you want to get it cut?

_____

2. When do you want to get it cut? (after school? Saturday?)

_____

3. What is the phone number of the store?

_____

4. When can you get an appointment?

_____

5. Do you want other services besides a cut? (wash, style, color, perm) What?

_____

6. How much will it cost?

_____

7. Describe how you want your hair to look when you are finished.

_____

_____

8. How are you going to get there and back?

_____

_____

BUYING A BIRTHDAY CARD

Objective:

Given the problem of having to purchase a birthday card, the student will identify a likely community resource and appropriate procedures to solve the problem.

Discussion:

Teacher: Today, I want you to figure out what you would do to get a birthday card for your mother. Let's say you have $2.00 in your pocket to spend. By now you know what to think about—where you could go, where to look in the store, and how to pay for it. Where are some stores close by where you could get a birthday card?

    Worksheet III-101 First, fill in the name of the store where you would like to get your mother a card. Then, answer the questions on the worksheet by writing *yes* or *no.*

Answers:

1. No	4. No
2. Yes	5. Yes
3. No	6. Yes

Extension Activities:

1. **Special Occasion Buying.** Enlist the cooperation of parents and pick out a special occasion that could require the purchase of a card. Have students determine the specifics of the type of card they should buy, for example, for a birthday, anniversary, 4-year-old, father, and so on, and actually go through the process of making the purchase. Have the class evaluate whether or not the student wisely selected an appropriate card.

2. **Buying a Birthday Gift.** Extend this activity by having the student decide what type of gift would be appropriate for a selected person/occasion. Determine an appropriate amount of money ($3.00–5.00) and have the student consider two or three items before making the purchase. Discuss why the selected gift was chosen, and what steps were involved in making the purchase. Incorporate parental involvement in this activity if possible.

III–101

BUYING A BIRTHDAY CARD

Your dad just dropped you off in front of the store that you said you wanted to go to. Now—what will you do to get that birthday card? Write *yes* or *no* next to each situation.

STORE: _____

1. You enter the store and head straight for the toy section, hoping you'll find something for under $2.00! _____

2. You look for the section that sells paper, stationery, gift wrap, and cards. _____

3. You find a nice card with flowers on it that says "Happy Birthday to a Nice Sister." You get it. _____

4. You find a colorful card with balloons on it that says, "To a Sweet 7-Year-Old." You get it. _____

5. You find a pretty card that says just "Happy Birthday" on it. You get it if you like it. _____

6. You take the card and the envelope to the cashier and wait for your change. _____

BUYING STAMPS

Objective:

Given the problem of having to buy stamps at a local post office, the student will identify appropriate procedures to accomplish this task.

Discussion:

Teacher: I just paid my bills for this month. How many stamps do you think I will need? (many) Well, my problem for the day is getting these letters stamped and mailed. How much does a stamp cost these days? (answer may vary) Where can you get stamps? (post office or by mail) Your task today is to figure out how you would buy stamps at the post office. Does anyone know the difference between local mail delivery and out-of-town? Who can give examples of each?

Worksheet III-102 This worksheet shows a picture of people at their post office. They could be in line for many different reasons, but I want you to think about buying stamps. Go through the numbers 1–5 and then match the steps at the bottom in the correct order.

Answers:

4, 1, 3, 5, 2

Extension Activities:

1. **Post Office Tour.** Most post offices are happy to provide guided tours of their facilities and services. Students may not be aware of the many different activities that go on behind the scenes. Arrange for a tour.

2. **Mailing a Package.** This activity is a bit more involved than simply buying stamps, but with parent cooperation have students go through the process of taking in a package, telling the clerk "first class" or "parcel post," giving money and receiving change.

BUYING STAMPS

Here are the steps for buying stamps and mailing a letter at the post office, but they are mixed up. Look at the picture and use the clues to help you number the steps in the correct order. Write the number next to the correct step.

Put the stamp on the letter. _____

Go into the post office. _____

Give the postal worker money for stamps and wait for him or her to give you the stamps.
_____

Put your letter in the correct mail slot. _____

Wait in line for the next available person at the counter. _____

REPAIRING A BICYCLE TIRE

Objective:

Given the problem of having a flat bicycle tire, the student will identify a community resource that could provide the service of pumping up or repairing the tire.

Discussion:

Teacher: When you are an adult and drive a car, you might run into a situation of having a flat tire. What a chore to change it! Does anyone know what you have to do? (get a jack, call AAA) Well, at least you don't have to worry about that yet. But what kinds of wheel do you use to get around? (bicycle) What happens when a tire on your bike goes flat? (get air, replace tube, replace tire) Today that's what you're going to have to find out.

Worksheet III-103 When there's a problem with a bicycle tire, there are several things that could be the problem . . . and several solutions. Match the student with the problem to someone or some place that could help them. Write the letter on the line.

Answers:

1. D
2. A
3. B
4. C

Extension Activities:

1. **All About Bikes.** Have students talk to local bicycle dealers and collect pamphlets, pricings, and other information about new and used bicycles. Since most students probably have their own bike (or access to a bike), use this commonality to bring up taking responsibility for keeping their bike in good working order, knowing where to get replacement parts, and knowing who is a reliable repairman. Many students may be somewhat proficient in repairing minor maintenance problems. Have students share what they know about bikes.

2. **Bike Art.** Have students work in small groups, each person contributing one portion of the drawing of a bicycle. Put the composite bikes together and display them. Students may be elaborate—adding lights, horns, interesting paint jobs to their bikes. Discuss parts of the bike, bike vocabulary, and types and makes of bikes. Let students brag about their knowledge in these areas.

III–103

REPAIRING A BICYCLE TIRE

These students are having problems with their bicycle tires. Match each student with the place or person who could help them. Write the letter of each place or person on the line next to the student.

1. Oh, no... it's flat. But I live one block away from a place that can help me put some air in it. _____

A. BIKES ~ Sales & Parts

2. I'm putting air in, but it's not staying. I think there's a hole in the tube. But I know where I can go to get a new tube. _____

B. MR. FIX-IT! Small Repairs

3. What happened? My whole tire is bent out of shape. I wonder if the person I need to help me is at his shop! _____

C. DAD

4. I've got the new tube, but I'm going to need help putting it in! I hope he comes home soon! _____

D. GAS STATION

AIR

Dear Parents,

How many times have you been asked to be a taxi driver—hauling your child to and form lessons, practices, events, and social activities? How many times have you said "no" because you just couldn't handle any more jobs!?

The series of lessons we will be working on continues our theme of community independence, but focuses on helping your child get around within the community, safely and responsibly. And, we hope, with an increasing degree of independence!

Our lessons will cover basic rules for pedestrian and bike safety, using public transportation, finding adult resource people who can help out with transporting and supervising students, and being extra-careful after dark. You can help carry out these ideas by insisting your child follow carefully specified rules about being on the street, being out after dark, and being a responsible bike-rider.

From time to time, we may need a parent volunteer to help out with transporting or supervising children who would otherwise be unable to participate in some important activities. Could you be involved to some extent? (details to follow)

Although it may be hard to think of your child as getting around independently, remember—the more responsible you child is now, the easier it will be later. As he or she learns respect for rules and the freedom that accompanies that respect, greater independence can be given—and that means freedom for you!

Thanks for your help.

Sincerely,

_____

Teacher

Skill Sheet #15: Progress Report

+ mastered
√ emerging
− not mastered

Student name	Pedestrian safety	Bike safety	Using bus	Parents, friends	After dark	Comments

---

PEDESTRIAN SAFETY

Objective:

The student will identify safe procedures for getting around on foot.

Discussion:

Teacher: Where are some places that you could get to "on foot"? (local shops) What does "on foot" mean? (walking) Does anyone know what a *pedestrian* is? A pedestrian is simply someone who is on foot. Whenever you are out walking on the street, you are a pedestrian. What are some situations that might be dangerous for a pedestrian who is trying to get around town? (traffic, being lost)

Worksheet III-104 This worksheet shows students who are walking around. Each picture shows a good safety rule that the student should follow. Write a good rule for each picture on the line below each picture.

Answers:

1. Walk facing traffic
2. Cross at "walk" sign
3. Stay on the sidewalk
4. Look where you're going
5. Ask an adult for help
6. Look both ways before crossing

Extension Activities

1. **More Good Rules.** Have students list more pedestrian safety rules (don't dart out between parked cars, don't play in the street, keep your purse/wallet close to you, etc.) and illustrate them on posters.

2. **Walking Tour of the Town.** From a central focal point, have students devise (and go on) a walking tour of the town or main area of interest in the town. As they write out the directions to the various destinations, have them indicate "safety spots" where they, as pedestrians, should take care to follow safety rules for crossing a street, being careful of footing, or whatever. Students may want to publish a walking tour map for others to use and follow.

Name _____ Date _____

III–104

PEDESTRIAN SAFETY

These students are walking around town. What is a good safety rule that is shown in each situation? Write it on the line below each picture.

BIKE SAFETY

Objective:

The student will identify safe procedures for getting around on a bicycle.

Discussion:

Teacher: Sometimes people don't want to get around by walking. Why not? (too far, too long) What are some other ways that students could get around? (bike, skateboard, horse) Today we're going to concentrate on bicycles and bicycle safety. Do you think that bike safety rules are similar to pedestrian rules? (yes—have to watch out for others; no—more like traffic vehicle than walking)

Worksheet III-105 I bet you know a lot of bike safety rules already. Write one rule in each space around the bike on the sheet. You can use the clues if you need help thinking of some. Then we'll compare answers.

Answers: (examples)

Don't ride at night without a light.
Don't ride on the sidewalk.
Ride single file in a group.
Use proper hand signals for turning.
Stay on the side of the street, don't zigzag.
Wear light clothes at night.
Keep your bike in good working condition.
Follow all road signs, including stop signs and yield signs, cross railroad tracks
   perpendicular to the rail, wear a helmet.
Put a flag on your bike.

Extension Activities:

1. **Obstacle Course.** Set up an obstacle course in the parking lot of the school or other large, flat surface. Arrange pylons so that students must demonstrate control over their bikes by staying within the designated lanes, stop at a certain place, use hand signals correctly, and so on. You may want to have students act as observers/raters for other students who participate by riding their bikes through the course.

2. **Bike Trip.** Weather permitting (and if all students have access to a bike), arrange for a group bike outing to a nearby destination perhaps resulting in a picnic lunch. Parents should be invited to help supervise and ride.

Name _____ Date _____

III–105

BIKE SAFETY

What are some rules that a biker should follow? Write one rule on each space around the bike. There are some word clues to help you if you can't think of many!

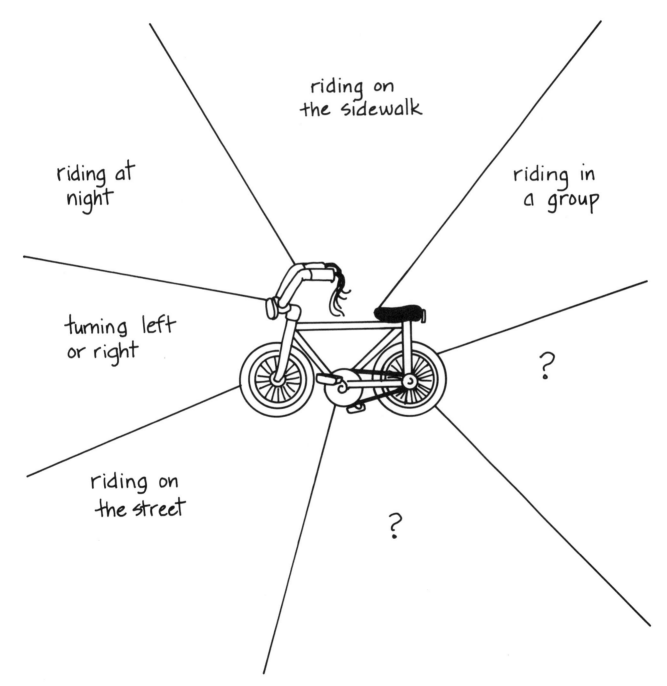

riding on
the sidewalk

riding at
night

riding in
a group

turning left
or right

?

riding on
the street

?

USING A BUS

Objective:

The student will identify steps involved in waiting for a bus, paying for the ride, departing at the chosen stop, and transferring.

Discussion:

Teacher: Many towns have a system for people to get around if they don't want to walk or don't have a car or whatever reason they may have. How can people in our town get around? (public transportation, bus, taxi) We are going to think about one type of transportation today: public buses. Who here has ever used the bus? Where did you go? Does anyone know of places in our town where the bus will take you? Let's find out more! How do you think we could get information about riding the bus? (public transportation department, bus station, bus schedules, other people)

Worksheet III-106 Here are some questions about riding and using the bus system. Some of you may know a lot more about how to use the bus than others, but it's good for everyone to know how the bus system works. First, you are to read the question and write down what you think is the answer. Then, after we have done some checking, we'll find out how it works in our town.

Answers: (will vary)

Extension Activities:

1. **Here to There.** Have students draw and color maps showing how they would get from a designated spot (school, their home, etc.) to a place of interest (zoo, museum, etc.). Have them write the specific steps, indicating the location of the bus stops.

2. **My Ride.** Have a student (with adult partner) actually go to a designated place using the bus. The student should record his experiences. Students will notice details that adults will not!

III–106

USING A BUS

Here are some things to find out about the public bus system in your town. In the first column, write what you think. In the second column, after you have done some checking, write what you found out.

Question	What I Think	What I Found Out

1. How much does it cost to ride the bus?

2. Do I have to have exact change?

3. Does the bus stop near my home?

4. What time does the bus start picking people up?

5. What time does the bus make its last run?

6. List three places that you would like to get to in town. Does the bus stop there?
   a. _____
   b. _____
   c. _____

7. Other questions:

PARENTS AND FRIENDS

Objective:

The student will identify other sources of getting around his or her community, specifically, people who can provide him with transportation or supervision.

Discussion:

Teacher: I want you to think about the last time you needed a ride somewhere. Where did you go and how did you get there? A lot of times there are organizations which have drivers ready to pick people up and take them somewhere. Can you think of any places that would do that? (churches, hospitals) Instead of always asking a parent for a ride, what are some other people who might be able to help you out? (older friend, relative) Part of being independent is being resourceful— that means using people around you who might be able to help you out without causing them a lot of trouble, like someone who is going where you're going anyway.

Worksheet III-107 Here are five students who need to get somewhere, but they each have to do a little searching to find someone who can help them. Match each helper person on the right with the student who could be helped on the left. Write the letter of the helper on the line.

Answers:

1. c   2. e   3. d   4. a   5. b

Extension Activities

1. **Volunteer Drivers:** Have students investigate the local volunteer center to find out which community places provide transportation, either by bus or drivers. Does the YMCA offer transportation to events? Is there a car pool coordinator? Does there need to be one?

2. **Helping Each Other.** Some students do not participate in healthy activities because they are limited by parents who work and cannot pick them up, or they do not have a bicycle, or perhaps they are not able to get a ride to get a physical taken for sports participation. Many adults, on the other hand, would be more than willing to provide an occasional ride for students, especially if their own son or daughter was involved. Often it is only the coordination of the need with the helpful person that needs to be developed. With parental help, devise a "network" of adults who are willing to be responsible volunteers to help out with these activities. (Check liability with the school and after-school leaders.) In return, encourage students who are the recipients of this courtesy to do a few local errands or yard work for the person who helped them out. Community independence does not mean total estrangement from any other person, simply being able to figure out independently a way to accomplish those community tasks that he or she would like to do—with or without other people.

III–107

PARENTS AND FRIENDS

These students need to get somewhere, but they also need some help. Match each student with the person who can best help them. Put the letter of the helper next to each student.

1. Rick needs a ride to the dentist's office, which is downtown. _____

2. Allen is supposed to go to football practice at the school field on Saturday. _____

3. Megan would like to go to a church in town on Sunday morning. _____

4. Sally has to mail a letter at the post office, which is about four blocks from her home. _____

5. Ben has a videotape that needs to be at the video store in an hour. _____

a. Mrs. Jones is going to walk to the post office to buy some stamps. She wouldn't mind taking someone with her, especially if the person is her next-door neighbor.

b. Jeff is an older brother who can drive. He would like to pick up a new VCR tape to watch.

c. Mr. Jones is driving downtown to do some errands for his business. He could drop someone off when he gets downtown.

d. Mr. Kelly drives a church bus on Sunday morning around the neighborhood, picking up people who would like to go to church.

e. James is a friend of someone. James's dad drives him to football practice every weekend.

AFTER DARK

Objective:

The student will identify ways to show personal safety after dark.

Discussion:

Teacher: We've been talking about how to get around to places in the community and finding people to help you. We've also been talking about safety in the community—being careful when you're out walking or riding a bike. Here's a new slant on things—how does darkness make things different? (have to be in early, can't see as well) What times do you have to be in the house at night? Why do you think parents and adults give you a time limit or curfew? (want you to be safe)

Worksheet III-108 On this worksheet, there are five pictures of students who are out at night or in the evening. In each picture there is someone or something that is helping to make that student a little safer. Circle the person or object that is helping the student be safer.

Answers:

1. Adult
2. Being in a group
3. Flashlight
4. Phone call home
5. Light-colored clothes

Extension Activities:

1. **Night Watching.** Have students assigned to observe other people in an evening hour. What colors are easily seen at night? What safe—or unsafe—behaviors have they seen? Have each record his observations and participate in class discussion the following day.

2. **Halloween All Year Long.** People become conscious of night safety usually on Halloween or trick-or-treat night. What rules or safety tips are publicized then? Which could be followed all year long? (dressing for sight, staying in groups, carrying a flashlight, etc.)

AFTER DARK

There is something in each picture below that shows how the student is careful to be safe at night. Circle the person or object that is helping him or her be safe.

4. Hi, Mom? I'm just leaving Kara's house right now. I'll be home in about 10 minutes.

Dear Parents,

Our next set of lessons deals with information that we find printed, posted, or folded in our glove compartments—schedules, directories, business hour signs, and catalogs. They are all sources of very helpful information, especially to one who needs quickly to find a bus route, a bathroom, or a store before closing!

While we will be working with samples at school, it would be very helpful for your child to learn to use directories as you encounter them in stores, the mall, offices, and even the newspaper to look up favorite television shows. Children need to know that information can be organized and found quickly if one knows the system—what a shortcut to random searching for that elusive store, or gift, or person.

Help your child by posing the question and having them help you figure out how to arrive at the answer. For example, when you arrive at the medical building for your dentist appointment, have your child find the listing on the directory. Then follow him or her as you ride the elevator to the proper floor and continue to follow systematically placed signs directing you to—the drill! Your child will enjoy being the leader while learning that information is supposed to make sense and be clear.

When it's time for the television to come on, have him or her look through the television guide from the newspaper or magazine and announce the evening's lineup. When a special show is announced for a later date, have your child make a note of it on the calendar and be sure to watch it together.

Practice *not* saying the answer! Let your child figure it out!

Sincerely,

_____

Teacher

Skill Sheet #16: Progress Report

+ mastered
√ emerging
− not mastered

Student name	Bus schedule	Menu	Tipping	Rest rooms	Maps	Mall directory	Business hrs.	TV guide	Newspaper	Catalog	Comments

READING A BUS SCHEDULE

Objective:

With appropriate information, the student will be able to locate a given bus route, times of arrivals, and important stops.

Discussion:

Teacher: Whether or not you use the bus system, it is still important to be able to figure out how it works in case sometime you needed or wanted to. What do you think you would need to know in order to get around by bus? (where to catch the bus, what time it comes, etc.) We have already talked about many of those things in an earlier lesson. Today we are going to work on reading a bus schedule. That will show you how to figure out which bus to take. Different communities use different bus schedules, but we are going to learn on a practice one, and then find out what works in our community.

Worksheet III-109 This shows a partial bus schedule for one route in part of a morning. Let's go over the information on the schedule together; then I want you to answer the questions below.

Answers:

1. W. Mill Rd. and 71st St.
2. 6:47 A
3. 7:41 A
4. 13 minutes
5. morning

6. not yet
7. 13 minutes
8. #3
9. no
10. #32

Extension Activities:

1. **More Practice.** Students may have difficulty understanding how the schedule works. Obtain local bus schedules and have students write story problems using the information. Students may want to personalize the problems using names of people in the class or specific occupations.

2. **Community Map.** As a special project, you may have a few students make a small model of major streets in the community, marked with bus stops. Using small toy buses, have students "run" the buses along a route, showing the designated stopping points.

Name _____   Date _____

III–109

READING A BUS SCHEDULE

Here is part of bus schedule for a community that may be similar to yours. Use the information on the schedule to answer the questions below. Write your answers on the lines.

MONDAY THROUGH FRIDAY		Route #32
Times given for each bus are arrival times at the bus stop.		
Leave: West Mill Rd. and 71st Street	Hospital Drive and Blumound Ave.	Ninth Avenue and Orchard Street
Stop # 1	2	3
6:32 A	6:47 A	7:10 A
7:13	7:28	7:41
7:45	8:00	8:13
8:19	8:34	8:47

1. Where is bus stop #1 located?_____

2. What time does the first bus come to stop #2?_____

3. If you got on the bus at stop #2 at 7:28 A, when would you arrive at stop #3?_____

4. How long of a ride would it be between stop #2 and stop #3 at 8:00 A?_____

5. What does the "A" tell you?_____

6. If you wanted to catch a bus at stop #3 and got there at 8:00, would there be a bus there?_____

7. How long would you have to wait for a bus (in question 6)?_____

8. If you got on the bus at stop #1 and wanted to go to Orchard Street, which stop would you get off at?_____

9. Would this schedule help you get around on Saturday?_____

10. What is the route number of this bus?_____

USING A MENU

Objective:

Given a menu, the student will identify prices of specific items and information pertinent to ordering.

Discussion:

Teacher: I'm thinking of something that helps you choose food when you're in a restaurant. What is it? (menu) What information is on a menu? (price, descriptions of food, etc.) How are the items grouped? (entrees, desserts, children's selections, etc.) Why do restaurants have menus? (so waitress doesn't have to say everything over and over, to advertise specials, etc.)

Worksheet III-110 Here is part of a menu from a restaurant that shows some items you might be interested in ordering. Look it over carefully and answer the questions below.

Answers:

1. 95 cents
2. Sandwiches
3. Two
4. Include more
5. Roast beef
6. Drinks
7. Entree, potato, salad
8. Desserts
9. Hot dog
10. Answers will vary

Extension Activities:

1. **Menu Math.** Using different menus from local restaurants, write items to make a meal on index cards. Have students use the menus to locate and total the price of the suggested meal. You could use duplicate copies of menus to have "food races" with competing teams racing to figure out the total first.

2. **Ordering.** Although students may go out to eat with family or friends, they may not actually practice ordering their food, but rather allowing others to order for them. In class, have students form groups and take turns being the waitperson and customers, using clear voices, eye contact, and decisiveness to place a food order. If possible, enlist parent support to take students out to eat at a restaurant, make decisions about meals, and order on their own.

USING A MENU

Here is part of a menu. Use the information to help you answer the questions below. Write your answers on the lines.

WELCOME * TO * JOHN'S HOME COOKING'

Beverages
coffee ....75¢
soft drinks ....95¢, 65¢
orange juice...................................55¢

Sandwiches
hamburger.......................................$1.35
cheeseburger $1.65
hot dog..$1.25
bacon, lettuce, tomato....................$1.40

Main Meals (All dinners include entree, choice of potato, and salad)
roast beef..$6.95
pork chops.......................................$7.35
baked ham.......................................$8.75
meat loaf $6.35

Desserts
cheesecake.......................................$2.50
hot fudge sundae............................$1.99

---

1. How much would a large soft drink cost? _____

2. Where would you look for a hamburger on the menu? _____

3. How many desserts are featured? _____

4. Why do the main meals cost more than sandwiches? _____

5. Which costs more, a roast beef or a meat loaf dinner? _____

6. What are beverages? _____

7. What is included with a main meal? _____

8. If they added chocolate cake to the menu, where would it be listed? _____

9. What is the least expensive sandwich on the menu? _____

10. What is something you would like to order? Figure out the total of your meal:

_____

TIPPING

Objective:

The student will identify types of services for which tipping is appropriate and be able to compute an approximate amount for the tip.

Discussion:

Teacher: When you're done with your meal at a restaurant, what do you usually get? (bill) You have to pay for your meal, but people usually leave some money on the table. Why? (tip, for waitperson service) A *tip* is extra money that you give to someone who has done some service for you, such as a waitperson. Can you think of other people who receive tips? (taxi drivers, hair stylists, delivery people) Most people tip about 15 percent for good service. An easy way to figure out the amount of the tip is to take the approximate total and multiply by .15 with a calculator or figure out 10 percent and then add half as much to that. For example, if the bill was $40.00, 10 percent of that is $4.00, and half of that is $2.00, so $4.00 + $2.00 = $6.00.

Worksheet III-111 On this worksheet are some examples of people whom you might tip if they perform a service for you or your family. After reading each situation, write who the person is (their role or occupation) and how much you would probably tip them. (Use 15 percent as a guide.)

Answers:

1. Waitress $1.50
2. Delivery person $1.80
3. Car wash attendant $1.20
4. Beautician or stylist $3.00

Extension Activities:

1. **It Costs That Much?** Have students use the menus from a previous lesson and tally the amount of the meal. Add to it the sales tax (whatever is used in your area) and the tip. How much does it really cost you to eat out?

2. **Good Service/Bad Service.** Have students interview adults to find out what they expect insofar as service from those whom they tip. What would a "good" waitress do that would warrant a larger tip? (friendliness, efficiency) What about a "good" worker for lawn care? (showing up on time, not taking too many breaks) Use the activity to teach a larger lesson that good work habits may pay off for them in terms of tips when they work for others.

Name _____ Date _____

III–111

TIPPING

Here are some people who have done a service for you or your family. If you were going to tip each one 15 percent, how much money would you give to each? (suggest using a calculator) Write the type of job or service occupation that the person is doing and how much tip you would leave.

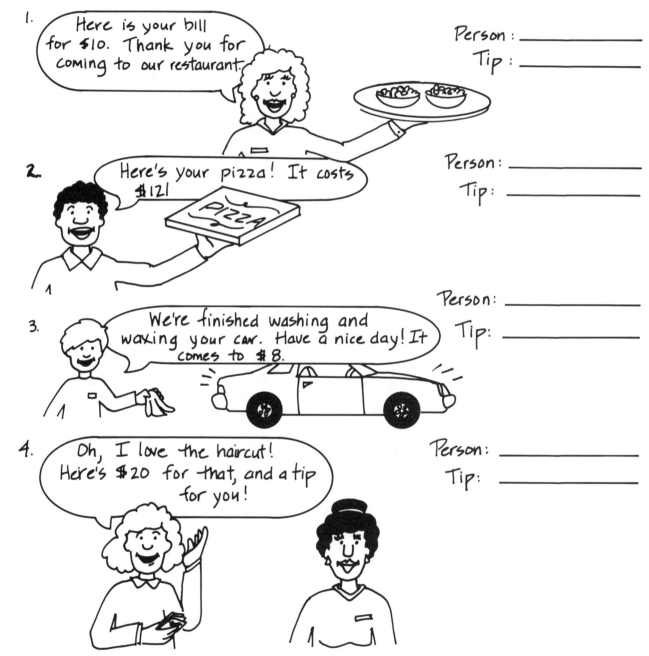

1. "Here is your bill for $10. Thank you for coming to our restaurant."

Person: _____
Tip: _____

2. "Here's your pizza! It costs $12!"

Person: _____
Tip: _____

3. "We're finished washing and waxing your car. Have a nice day! It comes to $8."

Person: _____
Tip: _____

4. "Oh, I love the haircut! Here's $20 for that, and a tip for you!"

Person: _____
Tip: _____

LOCATING REST ROOMS

Objective:

The student will be able to locate public rest room facilities in public or community buildings.

Discussion:

Teacher: Let's say you just had a quick lunch with some of your friends at the local fast-food hamburger place. You drank a large pop and a glass of water, and now you have to find a—what? (bathroom) Why do many public places provide bathrooms? (lots of people, too far to go home) Help me list as many places as you can think of that have public rest rooms. (should be a long list!) How are they labeled or how could you find them? (Men's Room or Ladies' Room signs, REST ROOM signs, Necessary Room)

Worksheet III-112 Here are two students, Sandy and Randy, who are looking for rest rooms while they are at the mall. Read each suggestion surrounding them that gives an idea for how they could locate the rest rooms at the mall. Circle the good ideas and put an X on the ones that aren't.

Answers:

Good ideas are 2, 3, 4, 6.

Extension Activities:

1. **Sign Collection.** Different places sometimes use different terminology to indicate rest rooms, especially restaurants (Sailors and Mermaids?). Have students be on the lookout for lots of different signs, wording, or pictures that depict rest rooms for each of the sexes. Don't forget the international signs, without words.

2. **What Would They Be Called.** Playing along with the idea of cute, creative ways to indicate men's and women's rooms, have students come up with rest room door signs for horse lovers (stallions and mares), Hollywood people (actors and actresses), hunters (bucks and does), et cetera.

LOCATING REST ROOMS

Sandy and Randy are looking for a rest room at the mall. Circle each way shown below that could help them. Put an X on the ways that probably would not help them find a rest room.

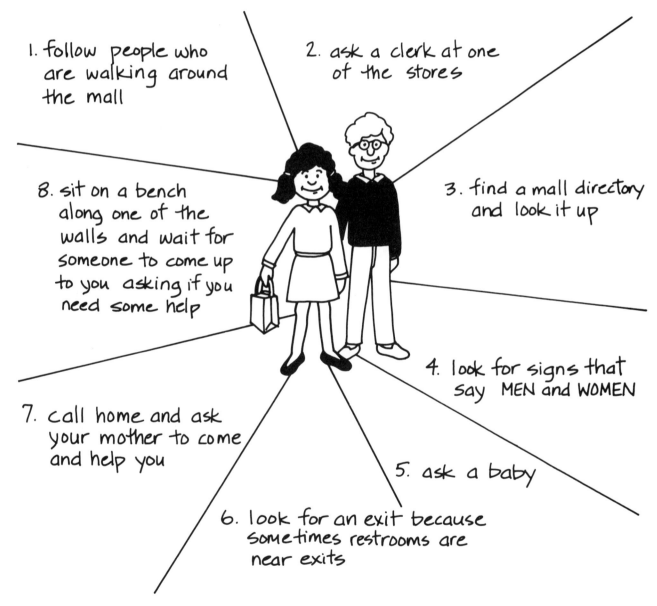

1. follow people who are walking around the mall

2. ask a clerk at one of the stores

8. sit on a bench along one of the walls and wait for someone to come up to you asking if you need some help

3. find a mall directory and look it up

4. look for signs that say MEN and WOMEN

7. call home and ask your mother to come and help you

5. ask a baby

6. look for an exit because sometimes restrooms are near exits

---

READING A MAP

Objective:

Given a map of a specific area, the student will identify features of the key and will be able to locate places on the map.

Discussion:

Teacher: I'm thinking of something, an object, that can help you find your way from one place to another. (If students say "compass," indicate that that points out only the direction they are presently going, not that that is the correct way or not.) It's a map! How many kinds of maps have you seen or can you think of? (road maps, state maps, world maps) What information does a map give you? (shows you where you are, tells what roads are there, the direction of specific places, where lakes and mountains are, etc.)

Worksheet III-113 This is a map of a community. Look at the compass to see which way is north. Now see if you can answer the questions about getting around using this map.

Answers:

1. 1st Street	2. Three	3. 2nd Street
4. 1st Street	5. North	6. North Lake

7. Start at the school, go west past Lake Drive and Zoo Lane; the zoo will be on your left

8. Turn right or east at the zoo entrance, go two blocks to Lake Drive, turn left or north and follow Lake Drive about two more blocks until you hit Pine Avenue. Go left and follow the curvy road until you get to the airport.

Extension Activities:

1. **Mapmakers.** Have students create their own communities by drawing a map and placing interesting sites within them. Students will enjoy naming the streets of their "subdivisions" and putting sports centers or animal shelters or other important community buildings on their maps. Then have students write directions or problems for other students, involving getting from one place to another. Be sure students include a key and a compass.

2. **Our Community Map.** Using a community map, have students solve realistic map problems, such as finding the best route from their home to the high school football field or locating class members' homes on the map and determining who is the farthest north, south, and so on. You may want to make up a thinking game, giving students clues as to which destination you are thinking of. Students will enjoy listening for clues that lead to their own house!

READING A MAP

Use the map shown to answer the questions about this community. Write your answers on the lines.

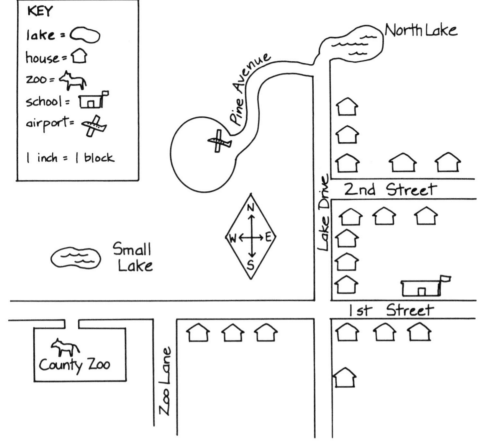

Questions

1. On what street is the entrance to the County Zoo?_____

2. How many houses are between Zoo Lane and Lake Drive?_____

3. Which street is north of First Street?_____

4. What street is the school on?_____

5. Is Small Lake north of or south of the zoo?_____

6. If you went north on Lake Drive until it ends, where would you be?_____

7. How would you go from the school to the zoo?_____

   _____

8. How would you get to the airport from the zoo?_____

   _____

USING A MALL DIRECTORY

Objective:

The student will locate various stores or mall areas by using a directory.

Discussion:

Teacher: How many of you have been to a mall recently? How many stores would you guess are there? If someone was new in our town and wanted to find a store there quickly, what could he or she do? (ask someone, use a directory) Sometimes when there are many stores close together or stores that have several floors for you to shop on they will put up a *directory.* A directory is a sign that lists all of the stores and services and where they are located. How do you think that might be helpful? (saves time, makes it easier to plan where you're going to go)

Worksheet III-114 Many malls put a large directory close to the entrance. This worksheet shows an example of a directory. Use it to answer the questions at the bottom.

Answers:

1. Two
2. Fashions and More
3. Bert's Flowers
4. Furry Friends Pet Store
5. 2-B
6. Designs by Denny
7. Johnson's Shoe Repair, Furry Friends Pet Store

Extension Activities:

1. **Other Directories.** Similar activities can be created by using office building directories (indicating different floors), department store directories (which may list stores by category, rather than name), and even a school directory, which may list the location of the various offices and classroom. If your school does not have one, offer to make one. (Helpful for conferences and open houses!)

2. **Directory of My Bedroom.** Have students complete a tongue-in-cheek activity organizing the items in their bedroom by location. Perhaps this could be hung on the outside of the bedroom door to assist parents who want to locate socks, yesterday's newspaper, important papers, pencils, and so on. Have students decide if they are going to divide the room into quadrants, enumerate items according to the perimeter of the room, use north-south-east-west directions, and so on.

Name _____   Date _____

USING A MALL DIRECTORY

Here is an example of a mall directory. Read it carefully and use it to answer the questions below. Write your answers on the lines.

WELCOME to SPRINGVILLE MALL!!!

B
Bert's Flowers... 1-A
Big and Tall Clothes... 3-B

D
Designs by Denny... 2-A

F
Fashions and More... 3-A
Furry Friends Pet Store... 1-B

J
Jenny's Cookies and Fudge... 3-B
Johnson's Shoe Repair........5-A

R
Restrooms...........RR

S
Silverman's Cafe...........2-B

1-A	EXIT	7-B	6B	5-B
2-A	X	RR		4-B
3-A				RR
4-A	5-A	1-B	2-B	3-B

EXIT

X = you are here

N ↑

1. How many sets of rest rooms are there?_____

2. What is the name of the store at 3-A?_____

3. What store could you go to to get flowers?_____

4. Which store has pets?_____

5. Where is the cafeteria located?_____

6. Which store is closer from the directory—Designs by Denny or Big and Tall Clothes?

_____

7. If you were meeting your friends at the south exit, what two stores would you be near?

_____

HOURS OF OPERATION

Objective:

The student will be able to determine what hours a store will be open by reading an "hours of operation" sign.

Discussion:

Teacher: What stores can you think of that are open 24 hours a day? (gas station, convenience store) Why aren't all stores open all of the time? (people need to sleep, may not be busy at night) If you wanted to find out if a store was open or was going to be open at a certain time, how could you find out? (Yellow Pages, call the store, ask a friend, sign on door) There are lots of good ways to find out that information—let's focus on one. What kind of a sign do many businesses put on their door? (sign that tells when they're open) A sign that tells when the store is open may be called an "Hours of Operation" sign or "Business Hours" sign. Why do you think stores put signs like that up on their doors? (so people know when to come back)

Worksheet III-115 On this worksheet, you will find two examples of stores posting their business hours. Use the information on the signs to answer the questions at the bottom. Write your answers on the lines.

Answers:

1. Thursday	5. 8 P.M.
2. No	6. Saturday
3. Monday, Tuesday	7. Sunday
4. Monday through Friday	8. Jewelry store

Extension Activities:

1. **When Are You Open?** Assign students to pick two businesses nearby and copy their hours of business. Analyze the information from the class. When are most businesses open? Do the weekend hours differ from weekdays? Do most stores have evening hours? Which stores? Arrive at some conclusions!

2. **Retail Versus Service.** Group local businesses into product/retail stores and services (dentistry, beauty salon, dog grooming). Assign students the task of phoning/interviewing the owner of the store or the provider of the service. Develop a set of questions including how were the hours of operation determined/are there more customers during the day or evening?/how many employees does it take to keep the business running smoothly? and so on. You may also wish to have a manager-owner of a retail store come to your classroom and answer questions about running a business.

III–115

HOURS OF OPERATION

Here are some business signs from two stores. Use the information to answer the questions below. Write your answers on the lines.

The Jewelry Store
WE ARE OPEN...
Monday 8 a.m. to 5 p.m.
Tuesday 8 a.m. to 5 p.m.
Wednesday 8a.m. to 4:30 p.m.
Thursday 8 a.m to 9 p.m.
Friday CLOSED
Saturday 8 a.m. to noon
Sunday CLOSED

Presto Print Shop
BUSINESS HOURS
Daily 7:30 a.m. – 4:30 p.m.
Sat. noon – 8:00 p.m.
Closed Sundays

1. You want to shop for a necklace, but you have to go at night. Which day could you shop at the Jewelry Store? _____

2. You wanted to get your ring cleaned, so you got to the store at 10 minutes before 5 on Wednesday. Was the store open? _____

3. Which two days have the same hours at the Jewelry Store? _____

4. On what days does the print shop open at 7:30 A.M.? _____

5. What time does the print shop close on Saturday? _____

6. On what day does the print shop have evening hours? _____

7. Which day is not a day of business for either store? _____

8. If you wanted to visit both the jewelry store and the print shop on Saturday, which store would you go to first? _____

TELEVISION SCHEDULES

Objective:

The student will use a listing of television programs to determine the time when programs will be broadcast, their duration, and the channel.

Discussion:

Teacher: What are your favorite TV shows? When do they come on? Why is it that you know those times so quickly? (watch them regularly) What if I told you that a special show was going to be on feature (someone interesting!) but I wasn't sure what night or what time it was on? How could you find out? (use TV listing, call a friend, check newspaper) Most newspapers publish information that highlights the regular shows and special shows that are going to be on each day. What information is given in this type of listing? (time, channel, information about it) We are going to practice looking up particular TV shows using a guide.

Worksheet III-116 This worksheet shows a partial listing of what's on television on a certain day. The left side tells what programs are on; the right side explains a little about some of those programs. Use that information to help you answer the questions below.

Answers:

1. Four
2. "The Day the Principal Went Away"
3. 18
4. 7:00
5. One-half hour
6. Shows famous places in Europe

Extension Activities:

1. **What's On Here?** Use a local television listing to have students answer questions about what's going to be on. Make a game by awarding teams one, two, and three points for correct answers to questions about the listing; for example, for two points, find out what channel has baseball on at 8:30 on Thursday, and so on.

2. **Movie, News, and Other Reviews.** Assign students (perhaps in teams) to view designated programs on certain nights during the week and report on them. Questions could be formulated beforehand, including (1) how long did the program last? (2) was it funny? (3) was it interesting? (4) how many commercials were there? and other pertinent questions. Make sure students circle their assignment on the TV listing and complete a report/summary of the show. Students may think that the news is "dull," but should give reasons why (*after* watching the news).

TELEVISION SCHEDULES

Here is an example of a television listing for a community. Use the information given to answer the questions below. Write your answers on the lines.

TUESDAY,   Nov. 13

Evening

6:00
(2) "Nightly News"
(4) "Local News"
(18) "Cartoon Friends"
(22) Movie Time

6:30
(2) "News" (continued)
(4) "Local Happenings"
(18) "Cooking with Fred"
(22) Movie (continued)

7:00
(2) "A Tour of Europe"*
(4) "Adventures with Math"
(18) "The Three Goofs"
(22) Movie (continued)

*Specials
(2) 7:00 "A Tour of Europe"—famous places to visit in Europe are shown in this program.

Movies
(22) 6:00 "The Day the Principal Went Away" (comedy). A high school goes crazy when the principal decides to take a day off to go fishing.

(18) 9:00 "Return of the Slimeman" (science fiction). A town is terrorized by an alien who resembles slime.

1. How many television channels are given in this listing?_____

2. What movie is on at 6:00?_____

3. What channel has cartoons at 6:00?_____

4. What time does "The Three Goofs" come on?_____

5. How long does "Local Happenings" stay on?_____

6. What is the special "A Tour of Europe" about?_____

ALL ABOUT THE NEWSPAPER

Objective:

The student will be able to use the newspaper directory to locate various types of information within the paper.

Discussion:

Teacher: How did the newspaper help you when you were trying to find out what shows were on television? (TV listing) What other information does the newspaper give you? (weather, local events, classified ads) For the next few days, I want you to bring in a copy of the newspaper so we can practice finding things in it and discovering all the different things that are available to us through the newspaper. (students whose families do not get a newspaper can share, or you can make sure extra copies are available) Why do you think communities print up newspapers? (information that applies to the area) Why wouldn't a newspaper from Japan help us find out what movies are playing down the street? If I wanted to know what stores were having a sale on shoes, how would a community paper help me?

Worksheet III-117 For this activity, you will need to use a real newspaper. Before we start, let's look through the different parts of the newspaper to get a general idea of what's inside. Then I want you to complete the worksheet, looking for answers in the paper.

Answers: (will vary)

Extension Activities:

1. **Newspaper Tour.** Most newspaper companies willingly provide educational tours for school groups, including brief descriptions of the jobs of the many people who are involved in reporting, typing up, editing, and printing the paper. This is a fascinating experience for students.

2. **Letters to the Editor.** Select a pertinent local topic (Should a skateboard park be designated for the community? Why aren't there more "G" movies at the local theater? etc.) and have students write letters to the editor expressing their viewpoints. Send them, with a cover letter explaining the project, to the local paper. Watch to see if some show up in print!

ALL ABOUT THE NEWSPAPER

Use your local newspaper to find the answers to the following questions. Write your answers on the lines.

1. What is the name of your newspaper?   _____

2. How many sections are in the paper? (usually indicated at the top)   _____

3. Where would you find the local weather? (section/page)   _____

4. What does the headline say?   _____

   _____

5. What is on television at 8:00 Thursday night?   _____

6. How many cartoons are featured?   _____

7. What pictures are on the front page?   _____

   _____

8. How many classified ads are there for cats?   _____

9. What movies are playing in your area?   _____

   _____

10. What coupons are in the newspaper? What products? Which stores?   _____

   _____

   _____

   _____

USING A CATALOG

Objective:

The student will use a catalog to locate information about items within the catalog and will complete an order form.

Discussion:

Teacher: I know a way that I can go shopping at a store that is 1,000 miles away—and I'll be back in 10 minutes. How could I do that? (catalog, phone order, TV shopping) You have some good ideas! What I'm thinking of is a special kind of book that lists all sorts of products. What is it called? (catalog) A *catalog* is a special book that contains a list of all the items that a store has or can get for you. How many different kinds of catalogs (or stores that have one) can you think of? (toy store, chocolate products, department stores, etc.) How is buying from a catalog different than buying from a store? (send away for product, might have to wait to get it, don't have to leave your house)

Worksheet III-118 This is part of a catalog from a made-up store called Crazy Joe's Weird Stuff. Can you figure out why it's called that? Read the descriptions about the items for sale and pick two that you would like to order. Fill out the order blank at the bottom, including sales tax (assume that it's 5 percent) and the handling fee. Total up your order on the very last line.

Answers: (will vary)

Make sure students correctly specify any color, size, or other features for the ordered items.

Extension Activities:

1. **More Orders.** Have students bring in catalogs from several different kinds of stores. Practice filling out order blanks, perhaps giving each student a $100 limit to spend on another member of the class. How much can they buy for their dollar?

2. **Our Class Catalog.** Have students draw or design an item or product, complete with brief description of its features, colors, price, and ordering information. Compile the items into a "class catalog" and draw up an order blank. What information needed to be standardized for the catalog? What numbering or coding system is used? How can they best describe their product in only a few well-chosen words? What makes a write-up appealing to a customer? Students will have fun creating and promoting their own "weird" inventions or ideas.

III–118

USING A CATALOG

Here is a sample page from a catalog. Pick two items that you would like to receive and complete the order blank.

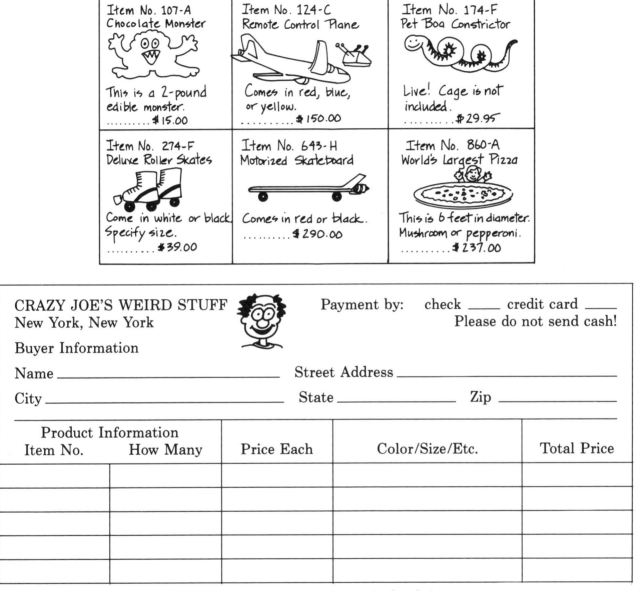

Item No. 107-A Chocolate Monster	Item No. 124-C Remote Control Plane	Item No. 174-F Pet Boa Constrictor
This is a 2-pound edible monster. $15.00	Comes in red, blue, or yellow. $150.00	Live! Cage is not included. $29.95
Item No. 274-F Deluxe Roller Skates	Item No. 643-H Motorized Skateboard	Item No. 860-A World's Largest Pizza
Come in white or black. Specify size. $39.00	Comes in red or black. $290.00	This is 6 feet in diameter. Mushroom or pepperoni. $237.00

CRAZY JOE'S WEIRD STUFF
New York, New York

Payment by: check _____ credit card _____
Please do not send cash!

Buyer Information

Name _____   Street Address _____

City _____   State _____   Zip _____

Product Information Item No.	How Many	Price Each	Color/Size/Etc.	Total Price

Order Subtotal _____

Sales Tax (5%) _____

Shipping and Handling:
$3.00 for orders under $20.00
$5.00 for orders over $20.00 _____

Order Total [   ]

part IV

Getting Along With Others

PARENT LETTER #17   RECOGNIZING DIVERSITY IN PEOPLE

Dear Parents,

The next major focus in our life skills studies is that of getting along with others. This is an area that touches everyone, everyday, everywhere. No wonder it is such an important skill to learn.

We will be talking about ways in which people are different in looks, jobs, personalities, and roles or responsibilities within a family. We want to convey the message to children that "different" doesn't necessarily mean "better" or "worse"; it's just what it says—different. Children learn prejudice as they grow up and are exposed to the viewpoints of others and experiences that affect their feelings toward others. It is important (for all of us) to judge people on characteristics that are not simply physical appearance or how one earns a living.

Listen to what your child says about others—his or her friends, siblings, people on television. On what basis is he or she making comments? Help your child understand that each of us has different qualities that can work together to help each other. A first step toward that goal is recognizing how people are different.

Thank you for your help!

Sincerely,

_____
Teacher

Skill Sheet #17: Progress Report

+ mastered
√ emerging
− not mastered

Student name	Physical character	Jobs	Personality	Experiences	Family roles	Comments

IV-A RECOGNIZING DIVERSITY IN PEOPLE   *LESSON 119*

WE DON'T LOOK ALIKE!

Objective:

The student will identify different physical characteristics of others, such as age, sex, race, physical coloring, and/or body build.

Discussion:

Teacher: I want each of you to think of another person who is in this room. Now think about how you describe him or her to someone who didn't know this person. Don't tell me who you're thinking of, but give me some descriptions. (list key words on board dealing with physical characteristics) Why do you think when we describe someone, we always start out with the way they look, rather than what kind of person they are? (most obvious characteristic, first impressions)

Worksheet IV-119 On this worksheet, you will see drawings of people who look very different from each other. I want you to describe the people you see using the physical clues or characteristics that we talked about. Try to use at least four words for each person.

Answers:

Tommy — Short, heavy, boy, white, young
Renée — Medium height, medium weight, girl/lady, white, young adult, blonde hair
Wanda — Medium height, medium weight, girl, black, young, black hair
Kim — Baby, boy, Oriental, dark hair
Lilli — Short, old, lady, white hair, white skin, glasses
Mohammad — Tall, man, dark-skinned, medium weight
Jennifer — Medium height, dark hair, glasses, girl, Oriental, braces
Luis — Short, Spanish/Mexican, dark hair, boy, young

Extension Activities:

1. **Who Am I Describing Game.** Have students take turns describing one of the people on the worksheet; other students guess.
2. **Body Tracing.** Have students make full-sized tracings of themselves. Add features to personalize the bodies. Include appropriate hair color, eye color, and other characteristics.

IV–119

WE DON'T LOOK ALIKE!

Describe each person below. Try to use at least four words to tell about each one.

1. Tommy

2. Renée

3. Wanda

4. Kim

Word Box

tall	short	young	old	medium-height
fat	thin	medium	girl	woman	man	boy
baby	white-skinned	dark-skinned	Oriental
glasses	braces	long hair	short hair

5. Lillian

6. Mohammad

7. Jennifer

8. Luis

DIFFERENT JOBS

Objective:

The student will identify a function of and characteristics associated with specific occupations.

Discussion:

Teacher: We talked about how people look different. Another way that people are different is what they do for a living. This is called an *occupation.* If I held up a piece of chalk, who do you think might use that on the job? (teacher) What is the purpose of a teacher? (to teach someone how to do something) What is the purpose of a police officer? (to protect others) What tools might a police officer use? (gun, squad car, etc.)

Worksheet IV-120 This worksheet is like a puzzle with some missing pieces. The first column lists some occupations or jobs. The second column lists what someone would do on that job or the purpose of the job. The third column lists some items that a person would need for that job. I want you to fill in all of the missing boxes on this sheet.

Answers:

1. Firefighter: to protect houses and people from fires
2. Secretary: typewriter, pencil, notepad, and so on.
3. : to keep people's teeth healthy/mirror, novocaine, drill, chair, and so on.
4. : to provide people with flowers for weddings, funerals, and so on/flowers, pots, and so on.
5. Beautician: to cut and style hair
6. Carpenter: hammer, nails, insulation, wood, and so on.

Extension Activities:

1. **Guest Speakers.** Invite people representing different occupations to talk about their jobs.
2. **ABC Game.** Have students think of an occupation beginning with A (auto mechanic) and continuing through Z (zookeeper). Then discuss the particulars of each job.

DIFFERENT JOBS

My Job	Purpose of My Job	What I Use
1.		boots hose
2.	type letters and answer the phone	
3. Dentist		
4. Florist		
5.		hair dryer scissors shampoo
6.	to build houses	

PERSONALITY DIFFERENCES

Objective:

The student will identify personality or temperament characteristics of people.

Discussion:

Teacher: Sometimes when you describe a person, the first characteristic is not how they look or what they do for a living. If I asked you to describe a witch, what might you say? (mean) Or if I asked you to describe someone who just gave you a million dollars, what might you say? (very nice) These are characteristics of someone's *personality*— what they are like on the inside. Let's list as many personality characteristics as we can in 60 seconds. (List may include outgoing, shy, loud, friendly, selfish, happy, bossy, kind, generous, etc.)

Worksheet IV-121 This page shows some students and tells you a little bit about their personality. What I want you to do is read (or listen to) the description of the student and write (or tell) a word that describes them.

Answers:

1. Selfish
2. Friendly
3. Shy
4. Mean
5. Helpful
6. Loud

Extension Activities:

1. **One Time I Felt _____.** Have students relate personal experiences describing a time or situation in which they felt extremely happy, sad, shy, and so on.

2. **Personality Poster.** Have students compile pictures of faces expressing different emotions and combine it into a large poster. Discuss why the people may be feeling the way they appear to be feeling in the picture.

PERSONALITY DIFFERENCES

1. Ronald never shares his toys with anyone. He grabs them away from other people and says, "MINE!" _____

2. Sally talks to new kids when they come into the class and don't know anyone. She knows it's hard to be new and not have any friends. _____

3. David doesn't like to meet new people. He looks down at the floor and doesn't say anything. _____

4. Claudia pulls people's hair and makes them cry. The she runs away laughing. _____

5. Kitty notices that a little girl can't reach the toys on the shelf. She picked the little girl up and helped her reach the toys. _____

6. Mike is always yelling, even when he isn't mad at anybody. "Quiet down!" the teacher is always telling him. "Shhhhhh!" _____

Word Box

mean	shy	loud	helpful	friendly	selfish

THE STORY OF MY LIFE: DIFFERENT EXPERIENCES

Objective:

The student will recognize that people have different pasts or experiences and will be able to relate a personal episode that is important in his own life.

Discussion:

Teacher: How many of you have two sisters, one brother, and a dog? How many of you have ever moved? How many of you have traveled on an airplane? How many of you can speak Russian? Not all of you are the same. Another way that people are different has to do with how they lived when they were younger and what their life is like right now. For example, if you lived in Russia, what language might you speak? If you were bitten by a big black dog when you were little, how might you feel about all dogs today? Can you tell a good or bad experience that may have happened to you when you were younger? Can you think of something about your life right now that is different from everyone else's?

Worksheet IV-122 This worksheet shows some students and tells something that happened to them. Read about each student and see if you can figure out how his or her experience might have made them feel the way they do. We will discuss your answers.

Answers: (suggestions)

1. Frank is afraid of cats. Perhaps Frank was scratched by a cat, saw someone else hurt by a cat, or is allergic to cats.
2. Sandy's clothes may be worn because they belonged to several people before her. She may not be able to afford new clothes.
3. Ramon may feel shy or lost or scared. He probably doesn't speak or understand English because he hasn't lived here very long.
4. Alissa could participate in relays that don't require running. She may have had an accident, but more likely she has a condition such as muscular dystrophy or cerebral palsy.

Extension Activities:

1. **Photo Time Line.** Students can bring in pictures of themselves from when they were babies to the present. Have them construct a time line using the pictures to indicate what important events happened in their lives.
2. **The Story of Me.** Have students write or dictate a short autobiography. This can be somewhat structured, if desired, to include specific points, such as where they were born, who is in their family, what places they have traveled to, what they are like right now, and so on.

THE STORY OF MY LIFE: DIFFERENT EXPERIENCES

1. Someone brought a kitten to school. Frank did not want to hold it. He did not want to come near it. When someone brought it toward him, he began to cry.

   How do you think Frank feels about cats?

   Why?

2. Sandy's clothes are worn. There is a hole in the elbow of her sweater. "It used to be my sister's sweater," she says. "Before that, it belonged to my other sister."

   Why do you think Sandy's clothes are worn and old?

   Why does Sandy wear them?

3. When people talk to Ramon, he acts as though he doesn't understand them. He is very quiet and doesn't talk much. The teacher says, "Ramon just moved here from a small town in Mexico."

   How do you think Ramon feels in school?

   Why do you think he doesn't talk much?

4. Alissa has braces on her legs. She gets around by using a walker. One of the kids in the class said that everyone should go outside and have races during recess.

   Do you think that Alissa could be included? How?

   What might have happened to Alissa for her to have braces on her legs?

IV-A RECOGNIZING DIVERSITY IN PEOPLE   *LESSON 123*

FAMILY ROLES AND RESPONSIBILITIES

Objective:

The student will recognize different roles that members of a family may assume.

Discussion:

Teacher: I want you to list or think about all of the people who are in your family. The members of a family might be the people who live in your house or the people you are related to. For right now, think of your family as the people who are part of your life on a regular basis. Now, let's do a quick survey: Who in your family does the cooking? Who takes care of the bills? Who works? Who does the chores around the house? Who helps others when they are sick? Who has to go to school and do home-work? All of these things are *roles* or jobs that members of a family have.

Worksheet IV-123 On this worksheet, you will meet a family called the Kellers. You will learn a little bit about the members of the family and the different roles they play. List the family member by the role or roles that they could have in each situation. There are lots of correct answers; be sure to give reasons for why you picked someone to do the job.

Answers:

1. Mr. Keller, Mrs. Keller (others are too young)
2. All
3. Mr. Keller, Mrs. Keller, and Beth; Tommy might be able to help
4. Beth, Mrs. Keller, possibly Mr. Keller
5. Mr. Keller, Mrs. Keller
6. Mr. Keller, Mrs. Keller
7. Beth (if she has a bike), Tommy (if it's close)

Extension Activities:

1. **My Family.** Have students draw a picture of the members of their family and describe each member in a few simple sentences, such as the worksheet. Discuss different roles within families.
2. **Chore Survey.** Compile a class survey of questions about who does which chore in a family. Does Mom always cook? Discuss changing roles.

FAMILY ROLES AND RESPONSIBILITIES

Mr. Keller works at a drugstore in the pharmacy department.

He thinks that children should do chores around the house.

He likes to cook.

He does not like pets.

Mrs. Keller is a teacher.

She likes to help children if they are having trouble.

She hates to cook.

She likes to drive.

Beth Keller is in third grade.

She does well in reading, but has some trouble in math.

She wants to take ballet lessons.

She loves animals.

Tommy Keller is in first grade.

He likes to ride his bike.

He is learning how to read.

He is afraid of snakes.

Who in this family . . .

1. could work at a job all day?_____

2. could do chores?_____

3. could cook the dinner meal?_____

4. could help Tommy learn to read?_____

5. could drive Beth to ballet class?_____

6. could help Beth with homework?_____

7. could ride a bike to the store for errands?_____

Dear Parents,

Continuing with our thoughts about getting along with others, we will be working on lessons about how people cooperate together and both sides come out ahead. We will particularly be talking about how people benefit from working together, playing with each other, learning, and developing friendships.

Help your child by using natural opportunities to point out how others help your family on a daily basis—the bus driver, picking up your child for school; the grocer, making many kinds of food available; the doctor, helping keep the family healthy. In return, what specific ways does your family benefit others? Talk about what mom and dad do for the family, for their employers, for the community, and for each other. *People need each other.* Sometimes the emotional-social needs that are met through other people are even more important than the basic physical needs. Point out how choosing good friends—and caring for those friendships through sharing and understanding (more to come in the next set of lessons!)—is very, very important!

Please continue to share with us at school if there is some specific task you would like to help out with!

Sincerely,

_____

Teacher

I-D TIME CONCEPTS

Skill Sheet #18: Progress Report

+ mastered
√ emerging
− not mastered

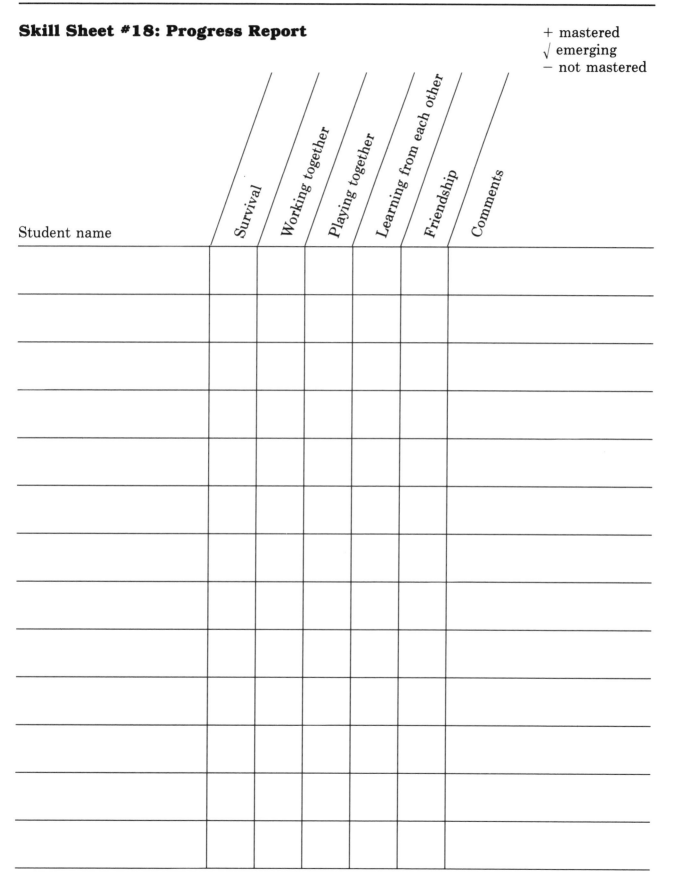

Student name	Survival	Working together	Playing together	Learning from each other	Friendship	Comments

IV-B RECOGNIZING NEED FOR COOPERATION   *LESSON 124*

HELPING EACH OTHER LIVE

Objective:

The student will identify ways in which the family structure helps the group meet basic survival needs.

Discussion:

Teacher: We are going to be working on some lessons that will help you to understand how people can help each other. First, what are the most important things that any person needs to *survive?* Survive means you have to have it or you won't live. Let's make a list. (include housing, food, air, water, clothing) How do you think people help each other survive or live? (working together, sharing things)

Worksheet IV-124 Here is the Keller family again. On this page they are getting ready for dinner. Read/listen to what each person is saying and list at the bottom which survival need is being talked about.

Answers:

1. Air
2. Food
3. Water
4. Shelter
5. Clothing

Extension Activities:

1. **Housing Needs.** Have students list and make models or collages of the different types of housing that people around the world use for shelter.
2. **Homeless Needs.** Discuss the problem of the homeless, particularly in your area. Be sensitive to children in your class who may be homeless. What can be done?

HELPING EACH OTHER LIVE

1. _____

2. _____

3. _____

4. _____

5. _____

IV-B RECOGNIZING NEED FOR COOPERATION   *LESSON 125*

WORKING TOGETHER

Objective:

The student will identify how workers of different occupations help each other meet their needs.

Discussion:

Teacher: Why isn't everyone a teacher? Why isn't everyone a doctor? (different interests, abilities, opportunities) If you had a toothache, who would you go to? (dentist) Why wouldn't you go to a person who sells cars? (not his area of training) Why is it important for there to be so many kinds of workers? (help each other, not everyone knows everything)

Worksheet IV-125 There are eight situations on this sheet that show how one person needs another person. Match the person who needs help with the person on the right who could probably best help him or her.

Answers:

1. D (banker)
2. G (gas station attendant)
3. A (teacher)
4. C (doctor)

5. H (server)
6. E (police officer)
7. F (carpenter)
8. B (travel agent)

Extension Activities:

1. **Job Fair.** Have students make posters of people working different occupations. Beneath each picture write captions: "I am a _____." "I help others by _____."

2. **What's My Line?** Play game in which one student selects an occupation and others have 20 questions in which to narrow down and guess the occupation.

WORKING TOGETHER

1. Mrs. Jones wants to keep her money in a safe place. Who will she see?

   _____

2. Mr. Carlson needs some gas in his car to get to the bank. Who will he need?

   _____

3. Jeff wants to learn to read. He will get help from someone in a school. Who will help him?

   _____

4. There has been an accident. A man will be taken to a hospital. Who will help him there?

   _____

5. The doctor is hungry from working. On his way home from the hospital, he will stop at a food store. Who will help him there?

   _____

6. The doctor was driving too fast in a hurry to get home. Who will stop him and tell him to slow down?

   _____

7. The banker wants to make his garage bigger. Who will he talk to?

   _____

8. Mrs. Jones saved a lot of money and wants to take a trip to France. Who will help her plan her trip?

   _____

A. Teacher

B. Travel Agent

C. Doctor

D. Banker

E. Police Officer

F. Carpenter

G. Gas Station Attendant

H. Server

HAVING FUN TOGETHER

Objective:

The student will identify several ways in which groups of people have fun together.

Discussion:

Teacher: Think about your family, friends, relatives, or people in your class whom you like to do things with, either at home or at school. Give me some ideas about what you like to do with others. (allow time for sharing) What are some fun things to do that you do alone? Is it more fun to do things with other people? Which things? When you do things with someone else, this is called *cooperation.*

Worksheet IV-126 Here is a list of ten activities which most children like to do. On the line following each activity, draw two smiling faces if you think it's more fun to do with someone else, draw one face if you like to do it alone, and draw both if you think sometimes one way and sometimes another. We'll talk about your answers and see what most people here like to do with someone else.

Answers: (will vary)

Extension Activities:

1. **I Had the Most Fun When . . . .** Have students draw a picture of a particularly enjoyable activity, labeling or mentioning the other people who may have been involved.

2. **It Takes Two.** Have students pair up and spend 10 minutes participating in an activity that one chooses (such as playing ball, working puzzles, drawing, etc.), and then 10 minutes in the other's activity. Discuss thoughts about sharing in an activity, even if it was not the student's choice.

HAVING FUN TOGETHER

Is this activity more fun with a friend?   alone?   or sometimes either?

☺☺   ☺   ☺☺/☺

1. Playing softball _____

2. Building a sand castle _____

3. Making lemonade _____

4. Jumping rope _____

5. Riding a bike _____

6. Shopping for shoes _____

7. Playing cards _____

8. Swimming in a lake _____

9. Canoeing _____

10. Working on a puzzle _____

LEARNING FROM EACH OTHER

Objective:

The student will identify activities or skills that can be learned from another person.

Discussion:

Teacher: What is something that you know how to do that maybe not everyone can do? Or what is something that you do particularly well? (allow time for sharing) How did you learn to do it? (another person, a book) Do you learn everything you need to know from a teacher in school? Who else can help you learn something? (friends, parents, etc.)

Worksheet IV-127 Here are some children who would like to learn how to do something. On the worksheet, circle all the answers that show someone who could help each child learn. Which ones would make good teachers? Some of the answers are silly, so watch out!

Answers:

1. Older sister, friend
2. Lifeguard, uncle
3. Dentist, mother
4. Friend, camp counselor, father
5. Neighbor, grandfather

Extension Activities:

1. **I'm the Teacher.** Have students take turns giving a mini lesson on how to do something that they are good at (drawing, taking care of a pet, skateboarding, etc.).
2. **Learning Something New.** Have a parent or fellow teacher conduct a mini lesson for the class showing them how to learn a new skill (origami, playing a new game, a few words of a foreign language, etc.).

LEARNING FROM EACH OTHER

Circle the answers that show who could be teachers for each child who wants to learn something.

1. Alison wants to learn to ride a two-wheeled bike.

older sister

dog

friend

2. Joey wants to learn to swim.

baby brother

lifeguard

uncle

3. Nancy wants to learn to brush her teeth.

dentist

mother

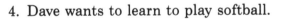
toothbrush

4. Dave wants to learn to play softball.

friend

camp counselor

father

5. Jason wants to learn to mow the grass with a power mower.

sleeping sister

neighbor

grandfather

WHAT IS A FRIEND?

Objective:

The student will identify characteristics of a friend or friendship.

Discussion:

Teacher: What is a good definition for a friend? (answers will vary) Let's list your ideas on the board. (You may want to group responses into "someone who does -" and "someone who is —.") Now think about your best friend. Who is that person and why is that person special to you? Let's say that a *friend* is someone who is good to you and good for you.

Worksheet IV-128 On this page are some sentences that describe what a person may or may not do to another person as a friend. Read/listen to each action and draw a smile on the face if you think it's something a friend would do. Draw a frown if it doesn't sound like a friend to you.

Answers:

1.	Frown	6.	Smile
2.	Smile	7.	Frown (some may disagree!)
3.	Smile	8.	Smile
4.	Smile	9.	Smile
5.	Frown	10.	Smile

Extension Activities:

1. **This Is My Friend.** Have students draw a picture, or bring a picture to school, of their best friend. Have them tell about their friend and why it is a good friendship.

2. **Friendly Award.** Give small awards throughout the week when you see an act of friendship shown in the class. Students don't have to be best friends (or even like each other) in order to be kind to each other.

WHAT IS A FRIEND?

Draw a smile on the face if this sentence tells something a friend would do. Draw a frown on the face if this sentence tells something that a friend would *not* do.

1. Tattles on you when you make a mistake

2. Helps you when you are stuck

3. Waits for you before going somewhere

4. Lets you ride his or her bike sometimes

5. Always wants to do things his or her way

6. Takes care of your dog when you go on vacation

7. Uses your skateboard without asking

8. Stops you from getting in trouble

9. Lets you borrow a shirt (if it's okay with his or her parents)

10. Is nice to you when you feel badly

Dear Parents,

Our next series of lessons on getting along with others is a lifelong learning process—trying to understand others, to leave your own point of view behind and see something from someone else's perspective.

We will be working on exploring situations from two points of view—not that one is wrong and one is right, but just two ways of looking at something. You can help at home by explaining unclear situations to your child and taking time to analyze the reasons why someone might feel differently about what to do with free time, the best way to settle an argument, or what is appropriate to wear when playing outside in the mud.

We will also be discussing arguments—how some of them start and continue simply because the two points of view don't understand each other. When arguments occur at home, help your child see that they can be settled justly (usually!) by reviewing rules, the situation, and what is or is not beyond someone's control.

Look for the worksheets your child brings home and discuss the ideas presented there. How were the situations settled in each case? Could it work in other situations? Emphasize common sense!

Thanks!

Sincerely,

_____

Teacher

© 1992 by The Center for Applied Research in Education

Skill Sheet #19: Progress Report

+ mastered
√ emerging
− not mastered

Student name	Another point of view	My mistake	Your mistake	Interviewing	Discussion	Argument	Defining terms	Common sense	Comments

ANOTHER POINT OF VIEW

Objective:

The student will be able to state at least two points of view for a given situation.

Discussion:

Teacher: Have you ever been in a situation where you saw something differently than your parents or a brother or sister? Can anyone give an example? (allow time for sharing) Sometimes people have a different *point of view.* That means they "see it differently" from you, but it doesn't mean either one of you is wrong. It just means there is a different side to look at. To understand others, it helps you see things from their side or their point of view.

Worksheet IV-129 This sheet lists some topics that not everyone feels the same about. For example, some people like these things; others don't. On this worksheet you will practice thinking two different ways to try to understand another point of view. Write in what you think each person might be saying.

Answers: (will vary)

1. Cats can be friendly and funny.
2. I am old enough and brave enough to ride.
3. I think that hair style looks great.
4. Bikes are safer in the street than on a sidewalk.
5. I eat lots of chocolate without getting fat.
6. It's mean to play phone tricks on people.

Extension Activities:

1. **"Yes, but . . ." Game.** Have students sit with a partner (back to back) and take opposite sides of a controversial topic. Others watch and give each side 30 seconds to state their side.

2. **Two Sides.** Have students fold a sheet of paper in half. On one side they should illustrate the "pro" side of a topic; on the other, the "con" side, or an alternate point of view. Students should discuss and select topics they wish to portray.

ANOTHER POINT OF VIEW

Each of the people here has a different point of view about the subject. One point of view is given. Fill in what the other person might be saying to show his or her point of view.

OOPS, MY MISTAKE

Objective:

The student will identify/demonstrate ways to handle a situation when he or she has made a mistake in judgment.

Discussion:

Teacher: Everyone makes mistakes. Can anyone tell about a time when you really messed up or made a bad mistake? (allow time for sharing) What did you do to correct the situation or make things right? How did you feel? Let's think of a *mistake* as something you wish you could take back or do over correctly.

Worksheet IV-130 Here are some examples of children who made mistakes. Let's go through each situation and think about what each person should do next to make things better. After you circle your answers, we'll discuss your thoughts.

Answers:

1. a, b   4. a, c
2. a (maybe), b   5. a, b
3. b

Extension Activities:

1. **Role Playing.** Have the students choose a situation from the worksheet and act out the problem and a chosen solution.

2. **Cartoon Problems.** Have the students think of their own mistakes and draw a cartoon depicting the situation. Have students brainstorm possible solutions and pick the best one.

OOPS, MY MISTAKE

These students have made mistakes. What could each do to make things better? Circle the letter for each answer you pick.

YOUR MISTAKE THIS TIME

Objective:

The student will identify/demonstrate ways to handle a situation when another person has made a mistake in judgment.

Discussion:

Teacher: Remember we talked about everyone making a mistake some time or another. Today we're going to talk about situations in which *you* are right and the other person made a mistake. Can anyone tell about a time when you were blamed for something you didn't do? How did you handle it? (allow time for sharing)

Worksheet IV-131 Here are some situations where you can pretend someone is making a mistake. How would you help that person stay out of trouble and keep yourself out of trouble too? Pick the first or second answer in each situation. Then we'll discuss why you think one is better.

Answers:

1. Second
2. First
3. Second
4. First
5. Second

Extension Activities:

1. **Role Playing.** Have the students select a situation from the worksheet and act out the problem and chosen solution.

2. **The Next Time That Happens.** Have students select a few situations that arise frequently in their everyday lives that possibly get them in trouble (fighting with friends, yelling at siblings, etc.), even when they aren't totally to blame, and decide on a course of action for "the next time that happens." Keep checking to see how it's working!

YOUR MISTAKE THIS TIME

How could you handle this situation if someone else made a mistake? Circle the best action.

1. Your mom thinks you broke her favorite vase, but it was your little sister who did it.

2. Your teacher marked an answer on your spelling test wrong, but it is correct.

3. A girl tells you that you're going the wrong way to get to the park, but you know you're right.

4. A boy tells you that it's all right to take money out of his father's wallet, but you heard the father say that the boy couldn't have any money.

5. Your best friend is having trouble on a reading paper and wants you to tell him the answers so he won't get a bad grade.

INTERVIEWING OTHERS

Objective:

The student will devise and carry out an interview of another person.

Discussion:

Teacher: One way to really understand someone is to ask them questions and find out more about them. This is called an *interview.* If a new person came into our class, what are some questions that you might ask him or her? What would you want to know? (allow time for sharing) I'll list your ideas. (might include interests, fears, idea of fun, where he lives, where he moved from)

Worksheet IV-132 This sheet contains some possible questions that could help you get to know someone. Use this, and the questions you came up with, to make up an interview sheet. Think about what you'd really like to find out about someone.

Answers: (will vary)

Extension Activities:

1. **Conduct an Interview.** Have students work individually or in pairs and actually conduct an interview of another student (older, a different class) or parent or perhaps a visitor to your school. Have them present their findings to the class.

2. **Interviewing Partners.** Have students devise an interview to be used with a classmate. Discuss how the questions they ask may be different from those used to interview an adult or someone they don't know at all.

Name _____ Date _____

IV–132

INTERVIEWING OTHERS

Make a list of questions that you would like to ask another person whom you don't know or don't know very well. Select ten questions either from the list below or add a few of your own.

Interests

What's your favorite sport?

What do you like to do for fun?

Do you like to read? What kinds of books?

Do you have any hobbies? What?

What could you teach us about?

Personal

When's your birthday?

How old are you?

Where did you grow up?

Who is in your family?

Do you work or have a job? (if an adult)

Opinions

What do you think about school?

What is the scariest thing that ever happened to you?

What do you think about our principal?

What do you think about smoking and drugs?

Did you like a book/a movie/a game/an event at school?

HAVING A DISCUSSION

Objective:

The student will identify and explain key elements of a discussion between two parties.

Discussion:

Teacher: In an interview, one person asks most of the questions and the other person answers. In a *discussion,* both people talk and ask questions and try to understand each other. Let's make a list of some topics that you would like to discuss or talk about. What are your favorite things to talk to friends about? (allow time for sharing, list on the board)

Worksheet IV-133 Here are three examples of students trying to have a discussion. What should you look for in a discussion? (read over the four rules) Decide whether or not the students are having a good discussion.

Answers:

1. Yes—Topic: monster movies
2. No—No single topic, both sides talked, but didn't listen to each other.
3. No—Topic: baseball game, only one side talked.

Extension Activities:

1. **Let's Talk.** Have students list interesting topics and randomly assign them to pairs. Have them carry out a discussion for 1 minute in front of the class. Go through the four rules to evaluate how good their discussion was. Also have the class evaluate the discussion. Did both sides talk and listen? Can each person accurately summarize what was said?

2. **What Do You Think?** Tape examples of discussion from TV programs using a VCR. Have students evaluate different types of discussions. (Examples may be from soap operas, talk shows, situation comedies, etc.)

Name _____   Date _____

IV–133

HAVING A DISCUSSION

Rules for having a discussion:

1. Pick a topic.

2. Both sides talk.

3. Both sides listen.

4. Both sides understand the other side.

These students are trying to have a discussion. Go through the four rules for having a discussion and decide which groups are having a good discussion. Circle Yes or No.

1.

I like monster movies.

Did you see "The Creature from the Basement"?

Yes, it was great. Did you see "My Mother Is a Mummy"?

No, but maybe we can go this weekend.

Topic _____   Good Discussion? yes no

2.

Let's skateboard.

My brother is such a jerk.

Come on, let's go.

Do you like my new shoes?

Topic _____   Good Discussion? yes no

3.

I have tickets to the baseball game on Saturday. I'd love to go! I really like baseball! When I'm older I am going to play professionally. Well, I hope so. Well, I have to go! Bye!

Topic _____   Good Discussion? yes no

319

HAVING AN ARGUMENT

Objective:

The student will identify how an argument differs from a discussion between two parties.

Discussion:

Teacher: In a discussion, both sides try to understand how the other feels and listen to what each has to say. The term "argument" can mean different things, and not all of the meanings are bad. For our purposes in getting along with others, though, we will use the word *argument* to describe a situation in which there is not good listening and good understanding going on, or there is disagreement without good reasons. What are some things that you might argue about with a friend? with a parent?

Worksheet IV-134 On this sheet you will find some examples of people having arguments. Let's read over some characteristics of arguments. (Read over the four points.) Decide which of them are involved in the arguments at the bottom. Each may have more than one correct answer.

Answers:

1. 1, 4
2. 1, 2
3. 1, 4
4. 1 (although the mother may not be involved in the argument), 3 (discuss whether or not they think this is an argument)

Extension Activities:

1. **Discuss, Not Argue.** Have students role play the arguments on the worksheet, only change them into discussions. Help them demonstrate how the issues can be thought through by listening and communicating.

2. **Good Reasons.** Have students select "hot" issues that they find themselves arguing about with others and list various reasons why they feel strongly. Go through the reasons and clarify whether or not the group feels the reasons are valid or irrelevant.

HAVING AN ARGUMENT

In an argument . . .

1. Someone disagrees.

2. Reasons may not be very good.

3. Each side may not listen to the other.

4. Each side may not understand the other side.

These students are having arguments. Which reason above explains why it is an argument? Write the numbers of your answer in each box in the picture.

DEFINING TERMS

Objective:

The student will demonstrate ability to clarify specified terms so that they are objective, not subjective.

Discussion:

Teacher: Many arguments start or grow out of discussions because the two sides involved aren't really talking about the same thing. If someone says, "You can have my old shirt," but later says he only meant that you could borrow it, could that lead to an argument? If that person said, "I don't want it back, you can keep it," does that make it clearer? Does the word "have" mean forever or just for a little while? What are some instructions that people give you that aren't always very clear? When you *define* something, it means you say it clearly so that everyone understands what you mean.

Worksheet IV-135 You will see four examples of people who are talking, but not really understanding each other. You will rewrite what the first person in each example is saying to make it very clear to both sides what they mean. (You may wish to do the first example together.)

Answers: (will vary)

1. "Come in in one hour."
2. "Ask your aunt how her trip was and sit quietly in the chair for at least 15 minutes."
3. "Play with your own toys. No hitting."
4. "Don't take anything or even touch it!"

Extension Activities:

1. **What I Mean Is.** Continue listing instructions that may not be clear (e.g., Dress nicely, clean your room, take a bath), and have students specify exactly what is involved in each instruction for them.
2. **What Happened Next.** Using the four examples, have students write or draw the next logical event that could happen based on the misinterpreted instruction.

Name _____ Date _____

IV–135

DEFINING TERMS

These people are using words that don't mean the same thing to each side. How could you rewrite the instruction to make it clearer?

323

COMMON SENSE

Objective:

The student will demonstrate ability to use common sense to resolve conflicts.

Discussion:

Teacher: Listen to this little story and tell me at the end what the boy should have done: It was raining very hard one morning. A boy got up, got dressed, and was getting ready to go to school. He walked past his umbrella, went out into the rain, and got all wet. Then he got to school, all drenched, and told his friend it was his mother's fault that he was wet because she didn't give him an umbrella. Whose fault was it that he got wet? If he knew about the umbrella, what do you think he should have done? What does the term *common sense* mean? We will use it to mean figuring out what to do without being told.

Worksheet IV-136 This worksheet shows some ways to use common sense. (Read over the list.) Decide which person in each situation is using common sense, and write the number of the reason in the box.

Answers:

1. Second student, 3
2. First student, 1
3. Second student, 3
4. First student, 2

Extension Activities:

1. **Silly Stories.** Have students write stories in which the main character does not use common sense. Exaggerations of this can be quite humorous (e.g., wearing a sweater in 90 degree heat, playing in the mud with wedding clothes on, and so on).

2. **But You Didn't SAY So.** For a set time limit (10–15 minutes), require students to say specifically everything they mean, allowing others to misunderstand and not use common sense. They will find that having to specify everything can be time consuming, ridiculous, and funny.

COMMON SENSE

These are ways to use common sense:

1. Think the situation through to what will probably happen next.

2. Look around you and see if the answer is clearly there.

3. Think about how this type of situation was handled before.

Which of these situations show a student using common sense? Circle the student. Write the number of the way he or she used his or her common sense in the box.

PARENT LETTER #20
DEMONSTRATING GOOD MANNERS

Dear Parents,

If there is only one behavior we all wish could be improved in others, it is probably that of showing good manners. Perhaps we are proudest of our children when they are polite to others without being reminded.

We will be stressing using good manners in all situations. Specific things will be shaking hands with someone when you meet them, using eye contact, helping others who obviously need a hand, including others in activities, handling rudeness graciously, and staying away from things that can get you in trouble, such as pranks or vandalism. Finally, we will emphasize simply saying "thank you" for any courtesy that is shown.

Help us at school by stressing good manners at home. Specifically, tell your child how you expect him or her to handle a situation. Most children don't realize that eye contact is a sign of respect and may hide behind their shyness for many years. If you expect your child to answer the door a certain way, teach him! Good manners are taught, not simply grown! Be sure to model the behaviors you'd like to see in your child as well.

This is the final section in our life skills activities. The lessons, however, go on throughout the rest of life! Please continue to help teach your child the skills he or she will need in life!

Thank you!

Sincerely,

_____

Teacher

IV-D DEMONSTRATING GOOD MANNERS

Skill Sheet #20: Progress Report

+ mastered
√ emerging
− not mastered

Student name	Courteousness	Meeting people	Movies	Helping others	Rude people	Including others	Vandalism, pranks	Cleaning up	"Thank you"	Comments

BEING COURTEOUS

Objective:

The student will identify situations in which courteous or discourteous behavior has been displayed.

Discussion:

Teacher: During the next few lessons we will be talking about being courteous. Does anyone know what that means? (being kind to others, good manners) *Courteous* means being considerate and polite to others. The opposite of courteous is discourteous. When you are in the community, that's different from being alone or with just your friends. How? (other people are around) Can you think of some community places in which you might be noticed by other people or have to talk to others? (library, playground, etc.) Why is it important to be courteous? (don't get kicked out of the place, don't annoy others)

Worksheet IV-137 This worksheet shows some students who are in community places. Some of them are showing courteous behavior; others are not. Write *yes* or *no* on the lines to show what you think. Then we will discuss your answers.

Answers:

1. No/noisy
2. No/mean remarks
3. Yes
4. No/pushy
5. No/inconsiderate
6. Yes

Extension Activities:

1. **Observations in Public Places.** Have students look for and report examples of courteous behavior that they have noticed in public places. You may want to put smiley stickers or faces on their drawings of good examples of good behavior.

2. **Today I Will . . . .** Have students discuss and commit to performing one specified courteous act to be performed at some community place that they will be visiting in the near future. It may be as simple as a polite comment, or a nonverbal act of unselfishness, or a secret card to cheer someone, but have them specify and predetermine what that act will be. Discuss how it made the students feel about themselves and how it made others feel. If it went unnoticed, was it worthwhile anyway?

BEING COURTEOUS

Look at the following pictures of students in community places. Are they being *courteous*? If yes, write *yes* on the line. If no, write *no* and explain why.

MEETING PEOPLE

Objective:

When meeting a person for the first time, the student will show eye contact, shake hands properly, and state an appropriate greeting.

Discussion:

Teacher: Who is someone that you would really love to meet? (rock star, sports figure, the president) If he or she walked into the room right now, what would you do? (run up, ask for autograph) Usually when you meet someone, or are introduced to someone for the first time, it's good manners to tell him or her who you are, shake hands, and say something like—like what? (examples: nice to meet you, how are you?) Today we're going to practice good manners when meeting someone— whether it's someone famous or just an ordinary person, you should show the same good manners. We're going to look for (1) eye contact, (2) shaking hands, and (3) something to say.

Worksheet IV-138 This sheet shows some examples of students meeting other people. You are going to circle the good examples and put an X on the examples that could be improved. Then we'll discuss your choices.

Answers:

1. O	4. O
2. X	5. X
3. X	6. O

Extension Activities:

1. **Handshaking.** Have students practice shaking hands with each other while maintaining eye contact. Teach them to grasp the other person's right hand (extended) and give a firm sincere clasp for a second or two. Students will probably be silly at first, but insist on this exercise when someone visits the room. You as the teacher may want to greet each student entering the classroom each morning in this manner.

2. **Students Meeting Students.** When students meet others of their own age, handshaking is probably not an accepted form of greeting. Discuss how kids can be friendly to each other and make a newcomer feel welcome to a group in other ways.

MEETING PEOPLE

These students are meeting someone for the first time. Circle the students who are showing (1) eye contact, (2) handshakes, and (3) something appropriate to say. Put an X on the students who need to improve in some way.

IV-D DEMONSTRATING GOOD MANNERS   *LESSON 139*

AT THE MOVIES

Objective:

The student will state ways that he could demonstrate good manners while at a movie theater.

Discussion:

Teacher: Has this ever happened to you? You go into a movie theater, have to jump over four people who won't move their legs for you to get through, and then end up sitting on a seat where there are popcorn and spilled drinks? How would that make you feel? (you wouldn't want to go back to that place) What's the point of going to a movie? (to watch the show) What are some ways that people can show good manners while at a movie theater? (be quiet, don't throw things, etc.) Why do you think some people *don't* care about their manners at the movies? (it's dark, no one will know who did it, takes too much effort to throw things away, etc.)

   Worksheet IV-139 I want you to think about what behaviors are acceptable or not at a movie theater. Read through the list and write *good* or *bad* according to what you think. Then we'll discuss your answers.

Answers:

1. Bad	6. Bad
2. Good	7. Good
3. Bad	8. Bad
4. Bad	9. Bad
5. Good	10. Good

Extension Activities:

1. **Class Movie.** Practice simulating good movie behavior by arranging the room in rows, providing popcorn (if desired), and showing an entertaining movie to the class. You may even want to have a ticket-taker, lines, and a refreshment counter. Practice good manners!

2. **Movie Behavior Review.** If students attend movies, have them fill out a "movie review"; they should rate the behavior of the other moviegoers, though, not the movie itself! Was the audience polite as a whole? What behaviors did they observe that showed good manners as well as discourteous manners?

IV–139

AT THE MOVIES

Read the following list of behaviors that could happen at a movie theater. Write *good* or *bad* to show what you think about that behavior. Write your answer on the line next to each example.

1. Getting up six times during the movie to go to the bathroom or use the phone

      _____

2. Saying "excuse me" when you step over people to get to your seat   _____

3. Laughing loudly during the movie, even when something happened that wasn't funny

                                                       _____

4. Throwing popcorn on some old people who are sitting a few rows ahead of you

      _____

5. Passing your popcorn or candy quietly to your friends ahead of you   _____

6. Letting your friends jump in line ahead of the crowd   _____

7. Throwing your empty cup and popcorn container in the trash can on your way out   _____

8. Putting your feet up on the seat in front of you   _____

9. Pushing through the crowd of people at the end of the movie so you don't have to wait to get out   _____

10. Sitting behind little kids instead of in front of them so they can see the screen   _____

HELPING OTHERS

Objective:

The student will identify specific ways to assist someone in a situation in which a person needs help.

Discussion:

Teacher: If you saw someone with a heavy bag and he or she were coming to a door, what could you do to help? (open the door) Do you think that person would say, "Get out of my way, I can do that myself"? (probably not) What would they say? (thanks for helping) Do you think people appreciate it if you help them when they need it? (yes—even though they may not say it) What are some ways that you have helped someone recently? Why is it good manners to do that? (shows you care about someone other than yourself)

Worksheet IV-140 There are lots of ways that you could show good manners by helping someone in need. On the left side of this sheet are examples of people who could use help. Match them with a person on the right who could help them. Write the letter on the line.

Answers:

1. d	5. b
2. c	6. a
3. g	7. e
4. f	

Extension Activities:

1. **Finish the Picture.** Have students draw a picture of someone in need of assistance, but without drawing a helper. Have students exchange pictures and complete each other's drawings by putting a person helping the first person in the picture (e.g., someone raking leaves, tying a shoe, etc.). The problem should be fairly clear before exchanging pictures.

2. **Good Manners Tickets.** Pay extra-close attention to students helping each other in the classroom. Surprise students by awarding them a small ticket (exchangeable for a small prize or candy) that says, "I NOTICED!" and tell them why you presented it to them.

© 1992 by The Center for Applied Research in Education

Name _____   Date _____

IV–140

HELPING OTHERS

Match each person on the left who could use some help with the student on the right who could help them. Write the letter of the student on the line.

1. Mr. Jones is very sick. The grass around his house is getting very tall.

2. Jenny is having trouble with her math homework. She has a big test on Monday.

3. The Kellers are going on vacation for a week. They have two cats and a big dog to leave at home.

4. Rick made an out while playing softball, and his team lost. He feels very bad about the game.

5. Grandma O'Brien has two bags of groceries to carry up to her second-floor apartment.

6. A man you don't know dropped a wallet while he was walking past the school.

7. A little girl has a letter to mail, but she can't quite reach the mailbox opening.

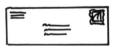

a. Frank could pick up the wallet and give it to the man.

b. Randy could carry the two bags up the stairs.

c. Alice could help go over how to do math and review the problems over the weekend.

d. Bob could borrow his dad's lawn mover and cut the grass.

e. David could take the girl's letter and put it into the box for her.

f. Jon could tell the person that everybody messes up sometimes, so don't worry about it, and then help him with batting practice.

g. Sandy and Megan could feed and walk the pets for a while until the family comes back.

RUDENESS IN OTHERS

Objective:

The student will state appropriate behaviors that could be performed when someone is rude to him or her.

Discussion:

Teacher: Even though you may have good manners, what should you do about people who don't? If you are courteous to someone, and they are nasty back to you—well, what could you do? (never be nice again, say nothing, tell them they don't have good manners) Let's think about some ways that you could handle a situation where other people are rude or don't show good manners.

Worksheet IV-141 On this activity, you are going to pretend you are with the person in each picture who is being rude to you. What would you do or say without losing your own good manners? Write or draw what you would say or do.

Answers: (will vary)

1. "I'm sorry if you thought I had it too long. Thanks for letting me borrow it."
2. "I guess purple isn't everyone's favorite color, but I thought the dress was cute."
3. Smile and say nothing.
4. "You certainly can borrow it if you need it, but please don't grab it out of my hand."

Extension Activities:

1. **TV Examples.** Have students watch a show on television and pick out examples of people being rude to each other. On some shows it is done to draw humor; be sure to point out that real life and television can be quite different. Even though it might be funny for someone to be put down for something about themselves, discuss why it could be cruel in real life.

2. **Good Examples of Bad Examples.** A quick response does not come naturally when someone has been rude to us; collect examples of rudeness in the classroom and make examples (anonymously) of how to respond to those situations (e.g., students rushing to cut in line, making fun of another student, taking items without asking).

Name _____   Date _____

IV–141

RUDENESS IN OTHERS

Pretend that you are the student in each situation shown here. Write what you would say or draw a picture showing what you would do. Remember to use good manners, even though the other person may not!

1.
Well, it's about TIME you returned my bike! I'll never let you borrow it again!

2.
So that's your new dress? I think it looks stupid and I hate the color!

3.
Young man, your hair is much too long! You look like a girl! Kids these days!

4.
Give me that pen!

INCLUDING OTHERS

Objective:

Given situations in which someone is left out, the student will identify the excluded person and state an appropriate method of getting the person into the group.

Discussion:

Teacher: Have any of you ever moved to a new city or had to go to a new school? How did it feel? Did it take a while for the strangeness to go away and for you to feel at home? What helped? (a person being friendly, joining a team, etc.) A way to show good manners to someone who is new or is not part of a group is to try to include that person in what you're doing. Why is it hard for some people to join in groups? (may be shy, not athletic, obnoxious) How could you help them? (ask them to join in, make effort to sit by them, etc.)

Worksheet IV-142 There are lots of reasons why people are excluded from groups—and most of the reasons are because we don't understand them or see their point of view. On this worksheet, show how you could help someone be included in a group if you were part of the group and wanted to show good manners.

Answers: (examples)

1. Invite Amanda to sit at your table.
2. Invite Ron to play for fun after school.
3. Ask Jaime if she'd take a look at your work or help you with something.
4. Spend time talking to Max; include him in games that he doesn't need to run around for.
5. Have a three-way partnership.

Extension Activities:

1. **Class Sociogram.** Have students in your class write down the names of their two favorite friends in the class. As you examine their responses, you will see clusters of friends in the class, and probably a few outsiders who are not picked for social activities. Without embarrassing the outsiders, encourage the more thoughtful members of the class to go out of their way to include them in activities.

2. **My Life as an Invisible Person.** Have students write short stories about what would happen to them in a day if they were completely invisible to all of their friends, yet able to hear and see what was going on. How would they feel if they wanted to join a group but were unable to, or were forgotten by their "friends" who ignored them? Point out that some people in real life probably feel as though they are invisible as far as being members of a group is concerned. Who in your class has that extra insight to find and help those outsiders? Look for stories that depict thoughtful behavior and read them to the class.

INCLUDING OTHERS

Here are some students who are not included in a group that they may like to be part of. What could you do in each case to help that person become part of a group? Write your answer next to each picture.

1. Amanda is new in school. Her family just moved from a long way away, and she doesn't know anyone. She sits alone at lunch and walks to school alone.

   _____

   _____

2. Ron likes to play football, but he's not very good and he's kind of short. He would like to play just for fun.

   _____

   _____

3. Jaime is very smart—she gets good grades without even trying. A lot of the kids don't like her because she seems stuck-up, but she has never been nasty to you.

   _____

   _____

4. Max is handicapped and in a wheelchair. Some of the kids in your class think there is something weird about him, and they stay away from him.

   _____

   _____

5. Everyone in your class has a partner for an art contest except Emily, who is very quiet. No one picked her to be a partner.

   _____

   _____

VANDALISM AND PRANKS

Objective:

The student will identify examples of vandalism or pranks and state reasons why such activity is harmful to others.

Discussion:

Teacher: Have any of you ever gotten a phone call and heard the person on the other end give a silly message? Or heard of anyone calling a wrong number on purpose and trying to tell the people that they have won a million dollars? Those kinds of phone calls might sound funny, but they can be mean, too. Why? (might scare the other person, older people might fear they will be robbed, wastes time) What are some other jokes or pranks you have heard about? What's vandalism? Vandalism is hurting someone else's property on purpose. It could also refer to public property. Can you give some examples of vandalism? (writing on walls, knocking over headstones on cemeteries) Why is that harmful to others? (someone has to pay for it, take time to repair it) Vandalism and pranks are not only bad manners, they can lead to seriously hurting or scaring other people as well as getting someone in trouble with the law. A joke is one thing, but when you tease someone to the point of possibly hurting them or scaring them, that is enough. Today I want you to think about why these things are wrong and how they could hurt others.

Worksheet IV-143 This worksheet shows some examples of people who are playing pranks or—worse—being vandals. This is a very serious subject, and we are going to talk about these examples together today. In each situation, tell how the people are being harmful to others and, second, what you would do in each situation if you were part of the group or knew about what was happening.

Answers: (examples)

1. The city will have to pay to have the graffiti removed, or people will have to look at the defaced bridge (also, the boys might be caught by police, especially if they write their own names!).
2. Mike will be in trouble for not having his work; he is worried about losing the papers.
3. Jane will probably feel very badly that she was made fun of.
4. The smaller boy probably needed the dollar for something at school; now he won't have the money for it.

5. Susan is being made fun of and is excluded from the group; by going along with the main girl's idea, the other girls are following a bad leader (and might find themselves being made fun of it they continue to obey her).
6. Stealing is a crime, and the boys could be in trouble with the police, getting a criminal record.

Extension Activities:

1. **Police Visit.** This is an excellent opportunity to have a local police officer visit and explain the consequences of vandalism on the individual, the family, and the community. Shoplifting is another area that should be addressed. Students should be made aware of what "breaking the law" means.

2. **Breaking Away from the Group.** Students should be aware that pranks and vandalism usually occur because more than one student or person is involved. Why? Why is it easier to do something in a group that you would never do alone? Discuss ways that you could pull out of the group or activity when you know it is wrong.

VANDALISM AND PRANKS

These people are involved in vandalism or pranks against other people. In each situation, tell (1) how it is harmful to others and (2) what you would do in each situation.

CLEANING UP YOUR MESS

Objective:

The student will state specific ways that the aftereffects of an activity can be organized to leave a clean space for another person to use.

Discussion:

Teacher: What does this room look like while we are working on art projects? (paper, glue everywhere) What if we just left the room like that and invited the class next door to come in and use our room to work on their math? (it would be hard for them) Can you think of other examples of when people leave messes? (eating at home, taking a shower) Why do you think it shows good manners to clean up a mess after you're done? (next person is entitled to a clean start)

Worksheet IV-144 It's lots of fun to get things out and work on them, but someone has to clean them up. It's good manners to clean up after yourself, especially at home where you share the space and materials with other people in your family. On this worksheet, circle the items that should be cleaned up or put away in each situation. Then draw a picture of what the area should look like when it's all cleaned up.

Answers: (examples)

1. Just the flower and vase on the table
2. Bike put away, everything else neatly stacked
3. Just the couch and the picture in the room, game in the box

Extension Activities:

1. **Before and After.** Have students pick an activity or area that tends to get messy. Fold a piece of paper in half and label and draw the area "before" you cleaned it up and "after" it's cleaned up.
2. **Surprise Your Mom.** Have students select one particular activity that they would like to clean up (without being asked) at home. Report results to the class.

CLEANING UP YOUR MESS

Look at the pictures. Circle the items that should be cleaned up and/or put away. Draw a picture of what the area should look like when it is cleaned up.

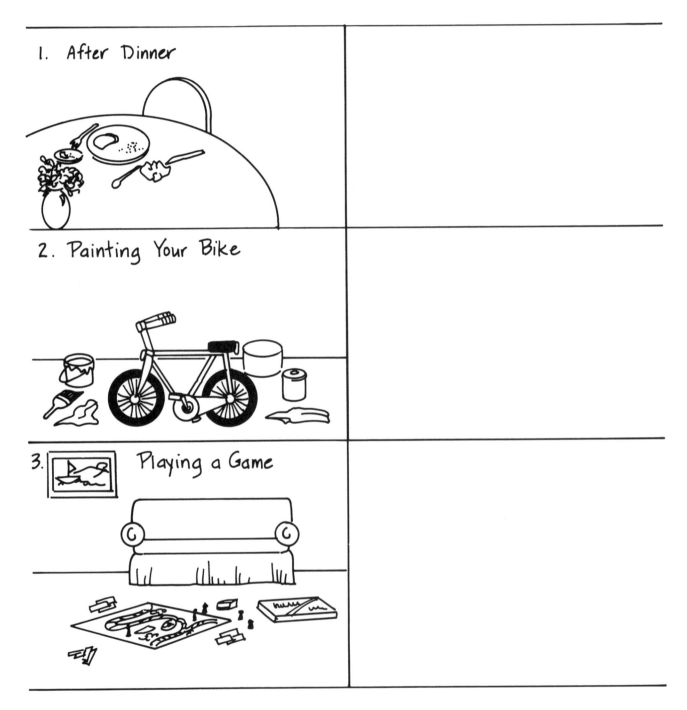

1. After Dinner

2. Painting Your Bike

3. Playing a Game

IV-D DEMONSTRATING GOOD MANNERS　　　　*LESSON 145*

SAYING "THANK YOU"

Objective:

The student will identify situations in which he or she should thank someone.

Discussion:

Teacher: I am thinking of one little thing that everyone could do to show that they have extremely good manners. It's only two little words, but it really shows politeness and courtesy. What are those words? (thank you) When you say "thank you" to someone, it makes them feel appreciated. Do you think they would be more likely to do something nice for you again? What are some times when you thanked someone? (dad helping with project, sister lending sweater, etc.) Do you think that if you thanked everyone who did something for you in one day, you would say "thank you" ten times? Fifteen times? Once? Let's find out!

Worksheet IV-145 Here are some examples from the life of a student named Ben. In each case, someone did something nice for Ben for which he should thank them. Let's talk about what he could say or do to show thanks. Does "thank you" always have to be said in words?

Answers: (examples)

1. "Thanks for letting me go first—you can go first tomorrow."
2. "You're the greatest, Mom!"
3. "Thanks, Frank!"
4. "You're nice; thanks."
5. "Wow! Thanks, Mrs. Jones!"
6. "I love macaroni and cheese; you're such good cooks!"
7. "Thanks—you guys played well too."
8. "Thanks, Aunt Sandy, now don't forget to send me a present! Just kidding!"

Extension Activities

1. **Many Thanks.** Have students go through their day (in a similar manner to the worksheet) and count up how many times they could have thanked someone. The following day, have them count up how many times they remembered to say "thank you."

2. **Special Thanks.** Select a person to be the recipient of your class's gratitude for some deed or activity or time spent with them. Have the students make cards, write notes, or throw a small party of appreciation. It is fun to be the *givers* as well as receivers!

IV–145

SAYING "THANK YOU"

A lot of people helped Ben today. Here are examples of some of the things that people did for him. In each case, tell what Ben could say or do to thank that person.

1. Ben woke up late, so his brother let him use the shower first.

2. Ben's mom made him toast and bacon (his favorite foods) for breakfast.

3. On the bus, Ben's friend Frank let him borrow his small video game.

4. At school, Ben dropped his lunch pail and a teacher picked it up for him.

5. Ben's teacher told him that he did a nice job on his reading paper.

6. At lunch, the cafeteria worker gave Ben a large helping of the macaroni and cheese.

7. At recess, Ben's team won at kickball and the other team congratulated Ben's team.

8. At night, Ben's aunt called to wish him a happy birthday for tomorrow.